Ada's Algorithm

How a Twenty-One Year Old
Launched the Digital Age
through the
Poetry of Numbers

James Essinger

GIBSON SQUARE

'[An] engrossing biography... that we might have entered the computing age two centuries ago had the contributions of Ada Lovelace been recognized in her time.'—**New York Times Book Review**

'A tantalizing topic… The story of a society proceeding irrevocably but ambivalently into the modern age, enthralled by advances in science and technology, adapting to new social mores, and yet still beholden to many antiquated traditions.'
—**Wall Street Journal**

'Essinger is a terrific storyteller, and he knows a great story when he sees it. Ada's Algorithm is a riveting read.'—**American Scientist**

'A fine new Lovelace biography… We need her as a symbol…of all the women who have contributed to the progress of science and technology, and of all the women who might have contributed if given the chance.'
—**Slate**

'Readers are treated to an intimate portrait of Lovelace's short but significant life along with an abbreviated history of 19th-century high-society London.'—**New Criterion**

'Irresistible … If more people could have understood Babbage's machine the way Lovelace did — indeed, if they had not all but ignored her paper, perhaps because the author was a woman — computing might have had a far earlier start.'
—**Chicago Tribune**

'A revealing firsthand look into Ada's life and her relationship with Babbage, relying heavily on their journal entries and letters to each other… One of the most innovative minds of the 19th century.'—**Boston Globe**

'Stepping out of the long shadow of Lord Byron's legacy, Essinger follows the visionary mind of Lovelace as she, applying her educated mind to the 'Analytical Engine,' creates the first recognized algorithm and casts a shadow on modern technology as long as her father's on poetry.'—**Biographile, Required Reading**

'[Essinger] presents Ada's story with great enthusiasm and rich detail… Ada continues to inspire, and by using her own voice via letters and research, the author brings her to life for a new generation of intrepid female innovators. A robust, engaging and exciting biography.'—**Kirkus Reviews**

'Absorbing… Essinger's tome is undergirded by academic research, but it is the author's prose, both graceful and confident, that will draw in a general readership. Readers are treated to an intimate portrait of Lovelace's short but significant life…along with an abbreviated history of 19th-century high-society London.'—*Publishers Weekly*

'The author provides an engaging…look at [Lovelace's] parents' romance, her childhood, her lifelong fascination with mathematics, and, mostly, her friendship with [Charles Babbage].'
—*Booklist*

'unfolding, generating a sense of place, time, drama and, at times, delectable gossip.'—*PC Magazine*

'The biography contains just the kind of moments of triumph I like to read about: Ada overcoming obstacles to get an education and make genius contributions to science.'—*Bitch Magazine*

'Essinger describes [Lovelace's] life with obvious respect, perhaps admiration, but also with a careful sense of journalistic objectivity and precision.'—*Geeky Library*

'A portrait of a particularly fascinating woman.'—*Jezebel*

'A window on the life of one of the world's first celebrity scientists.'—*io9*

'Anyone who thinks [Lovelace's] famous contribution to computer science is overrated, should read James Essinger's new biography... This concise and readable account gives Lovelace's work the respect it deserves.'—*Engineering and Technology Magazine*

'Entertaining and illuminating.'—*Times Literary Supplement*

'Essinger displays not only verve and affection . . . but also great scholarship.'—*Times Educational Supplement*

'The story [that] might have kick-started the computer age a century sooner.'—*Independent on Sunday*

'First lady of computers… what mark Ada might have made.'
—*Sunday Express*

'Appealing.'—*BBC Focus Magazine*

This book is dedicated
in friendship and admiration to

Dr Doron Swade MBE
&
Dr Betty Alexandra Toole

This edition first published in 2023 by

Gibson Square

Tel: 646 216 9488

rights@gibsonsquare.com
www.gibsonsquare.com

$\mathscr{C}$ontents

'You will not concede me philosophical poetry. Invert the order!
Will you give me poetical philosophy, poetical science?'

Ada Lovelace
writing to her mother
Annabella Byron
around 1845

$\mathscr{P}$reface

I became fascinated by Ada Lovelace while writing my book *Jacquard's Web: How a Hand-Loom Led to the Birth of the Information Age* (2004); at that time she was an obscure historical figure although she would pop up here and there. There is a break-through software language called 'Ada' that was originally developed by the US Ministry of Defence in the late 1970s to unite a host of different programming languages. Later, in 2009, the International Ada Lovelace Day was launched on London's Southbank to celebrate the achievement of women in science, technology, engineering and mathematics.

It would, at least at first glance, appear that science has a chequered record of treating women as equals of men. Indeed, female staff at Bletchley Park, the wartime decryption HQ that cracked German ciphers, were largely unrecognised for their painstaking work. Meanwhile Rosalind Franklin, who did much of the unrecognised Nobel-Prize-winning work on DNA, was ignored in all official recognition of the deduction of the existence of the double helix, to the embarrassment of the male scientists involved.

Whether this is historically a case of sexism or social conditioning of both genders is beyond the scope of this book. (Change is afoot for the future – as Lin Ostrom quipped on becoming in 2009 the first female Nobel Prize winner for economics, 'I won't be the last'.) What is clear, though, is that there is a surging interest in the history of women and their contribution to and involvement with science.

While Byron cast a long shadow over Ada's life, she was only six weeks old when they parted company for ever and so she never met him in any meaningful sense. The more important person was Lady Byron, who had been well-educated by her enlightened parents and moved in liberal circles. She maintained a ferocious control over her daughter's life and, as it would turn out, death.

The man with whom Ada Lovelace's story is most closely interwoven is that of her close friend Charles Babbage, the scientist who invented the first mechanical computer. Like Babbage, Ada was tireless in the pursuit of knowledge. She once wrote to him:

> I wish to add my mite [might] towards *expounding & interpreting* the Almighty, & his laws & works, for the most effective use of mankind; and certainly, I should feel it no small *glory* if I were enabled to be one of his most noted prophets (using this word in my own peculiar sense) in this world.

Their letters became so intimate that some think that theirs might have a been a romantic friendship.

Unlike Babbage himself, Ada Lovelace saw beyond the immediate purpose of his invention. He had little interest in that question and appears to have seen his invention as a 'mere' calculator. She understood that a whole new area of discovery awaited once the real world and abstract mathematics were linked through calculations that no human could ever hope to undertake. She speculated that such a computer, for example, might handle 'pieces of music of any degree of complexity or extent': a very familiar truth over a century and a half later but inconceivable to scientists at the time.

Ada was passionate, kind, imaginative, excitable and emphatic. She loved emphasising words in the letters and documents she wrote by underlining them (such words are italicised where she is quoted). She was in poor health and used mathematics as a way to regain her balance. She would later in life, when she was in serious pain, use medication that we now recognise as mind-altering drugs. After a long and excruciating deathbed that she appears to have suffered without complaining, she would die of cancer at the age of thirty-six, the same age as her father Lord Byron.

One of the fiercest criticisms of Ada is found in *The Little Engines That Could've* (1990) by Bruce Collier. This book, an otherwise shrewd and useful account of Babbage's work, contains much highly-informed technical material. But Collier writes this about Ada:

> There is one subject ancillary to Babbage on which far too *much* has been written, and that is the contributions of Ada Lovelace... It is no exaggeration to say that she was a manic-depressive with the most amazing delusions about her own talents, and a rather shallow under-standing of both Charles Babbage and the Analytical Engine... To me, this familiar material seems to make obvious once again that Ada was as mad as a hatter... I will retain an open mind on whether Ada was crazy because of her substance abuse... I guess *someone* has to be the most overrated figure in the history of computing.

Against this modern opinion one can let Charles Babbage himself give the answer. He wrote about Ada Lovelace on September 9 1843 to Michael Faraday, the nineteenth-century polymath who discovered electrolysis and magnetic induction:

> [T]hat Enchantress who has thrown her magical spell around the most abstract of Sciences and has grasped it with a force which few

masculine intellects (in our own country at least) could have exerted over it.

I hope that *Ada's Algorithm* will make it clear that Ada Byron, later Countess of Lovelace, Lord Byron's only legitimate daughter, should without doubt be included in the list of overlooked women whose potential was treated casually merely because of their gender. There has so far been no biography of Ada that fully defends the genius of her thinking, which prompted me to write this book. Ada's grasp of complex questions came with such ease that she was able to see beyond it where others needed to work hard to understand even the question itself. She herself called her area of thinking, in a letter to her mother, 'poetical science.'

The conversion of money from the past to the present is a highly technical subject. Its problems are discussed in some detail in one example. The conversions in this book are from www.measuringworth.com, which has a detailed and subtle discussion of the data and theory behind calculating worth over time. Ada Lovelace would have appreciated how its sophisticated calculations open up further areas of enquiry, an idea that was revolutionary two centuries ago.

$\mathscr{P}$oetic $\mathscr{B}$eginnings

Four miles south-east of the city of Canterbury, home to the great Norman cathedral famous the world over, you'll find the small village of Patrixbourne. Pretty and well-manicured, the village nestles amidst some of the loveliest countryside in the county of Kent, which has long been known as the 'Garden of England'. Among the many who have praised the county is Charles Dickens, who in *The Pickwick Papers* wrote affectionately of Kent's 'apples, cherries, hops and women'.

Today, on the outskirts of Patrixbourne, a muddy, rutted lane leads towards a large field featuring two long parallel rows of wellingtonia trees that date back to the late nineteenth century. The trees once bordered a long driveway. A few hundred yards south, a narrow stream called the Nailbourne – a local legend holds that it flows only once every seven years – is spanned by a little bridge made from stone and wood. The bridge dates back to the eighteenth century.

The wellingtonia trees and the bridge are the only signs today that there was once a splendid country house here known as Bifrons. The driveway led down to the house and in its day would have been used by horse-drawn coaches heading to the house or leaving it.

Bifrons, before being demolished in 1948.

As for the bridge, and the stretch of the Nailbourne it spans, these were once part of Bifrons' extensive grounds. Nowadays, though, the bridge is the only structure that remains on the estate.

Sixty miles from the smoky hubbub of London, Bifrons was an unlikely setting to have nurtured the intellectual development of the most famous woman in the history of technology.

Yet if you'd been visiting the house in the early spring of 1828 and had taken a stroll along one of the footpaths that passed through its grounds, you might have caught a glimpse of a pretty and precocious twelve-year-old girl called Ada Byron playing outside.

Ada had a turbulent and exotic background. She was the only legitimate daughter of the poet Lord Byron, in his day one of the most famous men in the world, notorious for his love affairs with both sexes, for the scandal of his passion for his half-sister Augusta, and for his disastrous marriage to Ada's mother, a well-born young woman named Anna Isabella, shortened to Annabella, Milbanke, who had married Byron on the morning of January 2 1815.

Patrixbourne in 1917.

When Byron married Annabella, he was already famous throughout Britain, Europe and beyond, as much for his amorous adventures as for his poetry.

Annabella put up with him for only a short period. During what was a nightmarish twelve months for her, but business as usual for Byron, the young couple were constantly harassed by creditors chasing debts incurred by Byron's fabulously extravagant expenditure on anything that caught his fancy.

The couple had a major cash-flow crisis because a dowry Annabella's parents had promised hadn't yet arrived. Her parents may have worried that once Byron got his hands on it, he'd leave her – and the dowry never did arrive during the one year and a fortnight that Annabella and Byron were together.

He himself regularly harangued his wife during the marriage with crazy outbursts, including declarations that she made him feel he was 'in hell'. He made love to Annabella whenever he could, but he was also comprehensively unfaithful to her, notably with his half-sister Augusta and an actress named Susan Boyle, though probably with other women too.

Augusta and Byron shared a father rather than a mother. Incest was by no means rare at the time, when poverty, overcrowding and cold houses meant that several people often slept in the same bed, even in large aristocratic houses. In fact, the aristocracy regarded incest between non-uterine siblings as reasonably acceptable. Byron saw Augusta as fair game. Augusta herself wasn't much concerned by the technicalities either. She just adored her half-brother.

Ada, born on Sunday, December 10 1815, was just over a month old when Annabella, having decided she could take no more of her husband, stole away with her from a sleeping Byron in the early morning of Monday, January 15 1816.

Annabella and Byron had made love on the night before her morning departure. Despite having fled her husband, Annabella initially retained some affection for him. She and Ada went to stay with Annabella's parents in Seaham, County Durham. From there, she wrote doting letters to Byron, but her parents heard how he had treated their daughter, and slowly turned her against him.

Details of the disastrous marriage soon got out, not directly from Annabella herself but from her lady friends. Annabella knew this, and had realised when she 'confided' in them that they would tell the world. Within a month after Annabella had fled from Byron, the disastrous marriage was the talk of the nation's drawing-rooms. Soon, fresh rumours began to circulate, that Byron had slept with Augusta during the marriage.

Byron, oppressed by debts, by the outcry over his marriage, and by his conviction that England didn't deserve a poet as great as him, departed from his native land on Thursday, April 25 1816, three months and ten days after Annabella had left him.

Even the sumptuous gilded coach in which Byron and his friends travelled down to the Kentish sea-port of Dover hadn't been paid for; bailiffs seeking the price of it were pursuing him. Byron's coach, a replica of one of Napoleon's, cost £500 at the time (£500,000 today), or at any rate would have done if Byron had paid for it. The pursuit soon grew more intense. He boarded a ship just in time, taking his luxurious conveyance with him. The bailiffs, with no legal right to pursue him beyond the shores of England, remained in Dover, staring out in frustration at the bubbling Channel.

The Channel was indeed bubbling as if heated by hellfire. Byron escaped his creditors, lovers, Annabella's wrath, Augusta, England and mundane reality in a 'rough sea and contrary wind', as John Hobhouse, a close friend from Byron's university days, reported.

The weather during the Channel crossing to Ostend, a seventy-five-mile journey, was so harsh the voyage took a nightmarish sixteen hours when it should have lasted less than half as long. During the long and horrible crossing, Byron – amidst bouts of seasickness – wrote the first three stanzas of the third canto of his long poem *Childe Harold's Pilgrimage*. The first two cantos had been published, to great success, in 1812. He scratched his anguish at leaving Ada onto paper as the furious waves battered the ship in the darkness, and as England, and all that England meant to him, receded into oblivion:

> Is thy face like thy mother's, my fair child!
> Ada! sole daughter of my house and heart?
> When last I saw thy young blue eyes they smiled,
> And then we parted, – not as now we part,
> But with a hope. –
>   Awaking with a start,
> The waters heave around me; and on high
> The winds lift up their voices: I depart,
> Whither I know not; but the hour's gone by
>   When Albion's lessening shores could grieve or glad mine eye.

Yet Byron's emotional convalescence didn't last much beyond his landfall at Ostend. When he finally reached the port, he celebrated his new freedom by seducing the chambermaid of his hotel room as soon as he had checked in.

George Gordon Byron, 6th Baron Byron.

2

ℒord ℬyron
A Scandalous Ancestry

The little boy fated to become Lord Byron the poet, Ada's father, was the son of John Byron, who had been born on February 7 1756.

John's older brother William – known as the 'Wicked Lord', whose crimes included stabbing a neighbour to death during a ferocious argument over the best way to hang game – held the title of Lord Byron, which was awarded the previous century to the Byron family by King Charles I. The Wicked Lord managed to escape the hangman's noose by persuading his peers in the House of Lords that the crime was manslaughter rather than murder. He was absolved from his crime on the condition he paid a fine and retired to Newstead Abbey in Nottinghamshire, the ancestral home of the Byron family. Founded in the late twelfth century, its priory status had come to an end in 1539, when it was closed by King Henry VIII due to his falling-out with the Roman Catholic church over his marriage to Anne Boleyn; he granted it to the Byron family.

John Byron, Ada's grandfather, was nominally a British army officer, but he spent as much time as he could philandering and spending money that wasn't his. These two pastimes had always been popular among the Byrons, who traced their ancestry back to a Ralph du Biron, who came to England in 1066 with William the Conqueror and his horde of fortune-hunters and land-robbers. John Byron soon acquired the nickname of 'Mad Jack'. Mad he might have been, but he was a handsome fellow. Before long he lost interest in his profession and in the family tradition devoted himself to dissipation.

John Byron's first wife, Amelia, had an annual income of £4,000 – worth £7 million today – which was presumably one reason why Mad Jack married her. Their daughter, Augusta Mary, was born in Paris on January 26 1784. She is an important character in Ada's story. Amelia Byron did not survive Augusta's birth, and the girl was cared for, most probably, by an uncle. The causes of Amelia's actual death remain a sinister mystery: sources vary between saying she died of consumption (this usually meant tuberculosis), of a fever contracted when she went hunting too soon after giving birth, or even of 'ill-usage' at her husband's hands. Some reports hold that her death took place in Paris, but her death certificate states that she died in London.

Whatever the true cause of Amelia's demise, her income died with her, and as Mad Jack had by now abandoned his military career, such as it had been, he needed cash badly.

In the traditional way of handsome aristocratic rakes who did not want to do anything so tedious as earn a living, Mad Jack ventured to Bath, a famous west-of-England spa town whose very name proclaims its primary historical function. The Romans had pioneered bathing in the supposedly healthy water. By the eighteenth century, Bath was still famous for its waters, and also for the opportunities it offered impoverished noblemen for finding a wealthy heiress.

Before long, Jack's good looks and easy charm had enabled him to do precisely that. The lady he successfully wooed ticked all his boxes of youth, wealth and vulnerability.

The lady, Catherine Gordon, was Scottish, a big girl and rather ungainly in her manner, though she liked dancing and was good-natured. Catherine was the oldest and by that time the only living daughter of George Gordon, twelfth Laird of Gight, Ada's grandfather. Catherine was born in the County of Aberdeen in 1764, and brought up in the Castle of Gight, which is in the parish of Fyvie in the Formatine district of Aberdeenshire, Scotland.

The exact date of Catherine's birth does not appear to be known, but she was christened on April 22 1764, and so she was probably born about a week before that.

Catherine had plenty of money due to her family inheritance. Mad Jack was as interested in Catherine's money as in Catherine, and indeed probably more so. The Byrons were not famous for the longevity of their virtue, or of their marriages. Soon after the happy couple were united, Mad Jack – relishing the prospect of living in a castle, and even more delighted at the juicy prospect of gaining comprehensive access to Catherine's money – began an orgy of spending.

Married women had few legal rights at the time and were not even regarded as a separate legal entity from their husband. Any money a woman had automatically became her husband's once they were married.

Poor Catherine – she would be poor soon – fell head over heels for Mad Jack, but only because in the classic fashion of rakes, he'd been careful to disguise his true nature until after the wedding.

Within a year of the marriage being solemnised, John Byron had spent most of his wife's fortune. Before she met him, she had about £22,000 (£35 million today). The inheritance rapidly disappeared, even to the extent of forests on Gight land being felled in order for the timber to be sold and the money to line Mad Jack's pockets for the brief tenure it had in them before being expended on some insane frivolity.

Within eighteen months of the marriage, there was almost no money left in the estate, and what was still there was paid to Mad Jack's new creditors because, in common with many of his Byron forebears, he wasn't only content to spend money he had, but also money he didn't. Catherine remained not only in love with her husband but infatuated with him. The scale of his financial extravagance, however, upset her profoundly. She was left only with the income from about £4,200 that her trustees had managed to sequester from her husband.

Before long, the threat of jail for debt induced Mad Jack to flee to Paris. Flitting off to the Continent was the usual Byron technique for dealing with debt. By the end of 1787, Catherine – unwilling, despite her persisting love for her husband, to spend any more time in Paris living in straitened circumstances – came back to London. Mad Jack couldn't join her in London because if he had, he would have been jailed for debt right away. By now, she was pregnant, and on January 22 1788, her son and only child came into this world. Catherine named him George Gordon, after her father.

The future poet Lord Byron was born with a caul, a harmless membrane, over his head. In medieval times a caul had been seen as a mark that a child born with one would be destined for greatness. Dried, cauls were believed to prevent their owner from drowning. Some were sold for significant sums to sailors. There is a reference to this practice in the opening paragraphs of Charles Dickens's novel *David Copperfield* (1850). There were no takers for David's caul, but baby George's was given to a professional sailor Catherine knew.

George was also born with a deformed right foot, which was to cause him both physical and psychological pain throughout his life. The deformity was at the time referred to as a club foot. Today, the condition is known medically as dysplasia and is characterised by the very problems that Byron suffered: his right leg was thinner than it should have been, and his long narrow foot curved inwards and was stiff so that it affected to some extent the movement of the ankle. Byron's walk, throughout his life, had a certain sliding gait to it which everyone noticed. All the same, this was a time when many people had something more or less wrong with them, so Byron's problem would not have been as conspicuous as it would have been today.

Catherine was deeply (and, based on his track record, most likely accurately) concerned that even now her husband, living in Paris, was accruing more debts. Certainly, the pressure on what money Catherine still had was apparently endless. Mad Jack was unable to get credit and was reduced to living only on bread. He was by now also dangerously ill with tuberculosis. On June 21 1791, he made his will, thoughtfully making his penniless son (four years old at the time) responsible for his, the father's, debts. Six weeks later, on August 2 1791, John Byron died at the age of thirty-five.

Catherine bravely contrived to manage on what money she had left. She sent George to a variety of schools in London. Finally she returned to Scotland and there, in 1794, when George Byron was six years old, he was enrolled at Aberdeen Grammar School.

Mad Jack's demented older brother, the Wicked Lord, was still alive at this point, but when he died four years later the ten-year-old George became the sixth Lord Byron. On hearing the news, the headmaster of Aberdeen Grammar School called George into his office, informed the boy of his momentous social elevation, and gave him a glass of port, as if determined to welcome the boy symbolically into the bibulous world of the aristocracy.

In 1798, becoming a peer was seen as becoming a new kind of being. Early in August of that year, Catherine and the ten-year-old Lord Byron, accompanied by his nanny Mary Gray, whom he called May, journeyed to Newstead Abbey, where he took possession of his estate. The boy was delighted with Newstead Abbey, and spent a month or so roaming the grounds.

Newstead Abbey, the ancestral home Lord Byron inherited at the age of ten.

Nanny May was woman of considerably loose virtue; she had regular romantic adventures with young men of about her own age, seventeen or eighteen.[1]

According to Byron's friend John Hobhouse – who later in Byron's life was told about these events by the poet himself – during this time when May Gray was Byron's nursemaid, she started taking the boy into her bed and masturbating him. Her interest in Byron, though, was not only that of a sexual initiator. She liked to alternate the masturbation with beatings; for which actual or imagined offences is not clear. May even enjoyed showing off to her male companions the power she had over Byron and she enjoyed beating the boy while they looked on. Very likely, the young Byron also witnessed the drunken copulations of May and her friends.

It was the beatings, not the masturbation, that young George Byron finally reported to his mother. When Catherine heard from her son that May was flogging him, Catherine dismissed May and removed Byron from Newstead Abbey. His education continued in London. At the age of thirteen, Byron entered Harrow School, at that time, with Eton, one of the two most renowned schools in Britain.

Life at Harrow was tough. You had to get up at six o'clock, and lessons continued for twelve hours, with some breaks for mealtimes. Floggings administered on younger boys by senior boys and by masters were commonplace; for the floggers, they were a high point of the school routine.

Academic standards could be high, but the syllabus was fairly unvaried. This was 1801, and the syllabus of Britain's public schools was mostly classical, with the intention of turning young men (there were very few schools that gave much of a classical education to young women) into proxy citizens of the great Roman Empire that had collapsed due to Barbarian predations about 1,400 years ago, but which still had an enormous cultural hold on the Anglo-Saxon mind. This was partly at least because the Britons admired the way the Romans had built up their empire: with violence, yes, but also with a genuine concern for the welfare of the governed.

One of Byron's school fellows was to become important in the life of Ada. This was the young Robert Peel, also born in 1788, though Peel was born on February 5 and so was Byron's junior by exactly two weeks. Byron was later in his life to be generous about Peel's talents.

Byron was prone to bouts of depression, and may even have suffered from a form of manic depression (nowadays known as bipolar syndrome). Byron himself often seems to have used sex more as a diversion and as a way of forgetting his own low spirits than necessarily always as a supreme physical and spiritual pleasure. He was in addition often curiously passive in courtship; when he reached adulthood and had many female (and male) admirers, they often found it frustrating that they themselves had to initiate things.

Indeed, Byron was also sometimes as intensely taken with chastity as with sexuality. His life's work fills a closely-printed book of almost 900 pages, and a man who spends most of his life indulging himself sexually and who dies at the age of thirty-six, is not likely to produce such a vast body of work – maybe around one million words in total. So while certainly Byron had bouts of energetic indulgence in sex, he wasn't always, so to speak, in the mood.

He was certainly bisexual. While at Harrow, he fell ardently in love with a younger boy called John Edelston. The social and moral atmosphere of Harrow was much of the time literally a hotbed of homosexual activity. The poet and critic John Addington Symons (1840 – 1893), himself bisexual, was one of the first to write explicitly about homosexuality in nineteenth-century Britain, when homosexual practices were still an imprisonable offence. Addington Symons wrote this in his memoirs of Harrow, which he started attending in 1854:

Every boy of good looks had a female name, and was recognised either as a public prostitute or as some bigger fellow's bitch. Bitch was the word in common usage to indicate a boy who yielded his person to a lover. The talk of the dormitories and the studies was incredibly obscene. Here and there, one could not avoid seeing acts of onanism, mutual masturbation, the sports of naked boys in bed together. There was no refinement, no sentiment, no passion; nothing but animal lust in these occurrences.

In the summer of 1808, Byron visited his friend Lord Grey de Ruthyn, who was about eight years older than Byron. Grey made advances to him which were evidently not repulsed. The poet and lyricist Thomas Moore writing in his own biography of Byron, said that an intimacy sprang up between Byron and Grey.

Byron liked to use the phrase 'pure relationship' to describe one which did not involve actual penetrative intercourse. It is not, however, known what 'intimacy' meant in terms of Byron and Grey. All that is certain is that Byron was himself conscious of his early sexual initiation. In 'Detached Thoughts' – a journal he kept for a few months in 1821 – 1822 when he was living in Pisa, Italy – he admitted:

My passions were developed very early – so early – that few would believe me – if I were to state the period – and the facts which accompanied it.

On Monday, July 1 1805, Byron travelled to Cambridge to become a student at Trinity College, the largest and probably the most famous of the colleges of Cambridge University. In Byron's time there was only one path to the degree, which was the Senate House Examination (SHE). The SHE was continually developing. At that time it was partially oral but mostly written, with the main subject of examination being mathematics, though a little classics and moral philosophy were thrown in too. However, most noblemen such as Byron treated Cambridge as a sort of finishing school and stayed only for one or two years, generally failing to graduate or even to make an attempt to do so.[2]

Byron certainly lived it large. He kept three horses and acquired a carriage soon after arriving in Cambridge. What he thought of the university was hardly complimentary. 'This place is wretched enough,' he wrote, 'a villainous chaos of din and drunkenness, nothing but hazard and burgundy, hunting, mathematics and Newmarket, riot and racing.'

Within less than a year of his arrival he had borrowed hundreds of pounds from a money-lender at a high rate of interest. Byron wrote to his impoverished mother that he had 'a few hundred in ready cash lying by me', and he then went on to tell her that he could learn nothing at Cambridge and would prefer to go abroad.

Appalled, his mother Catherine wrote to John Hanson, a young married London lawyer who had befriended her before Byron was born and even lent Catherine money when she needed it. It was John Hanson's brother, a Royal Navy captain, who had been given the caul in which Byron was born.

> That boy will be the death of me, and drive me mad! I will never consent to his going abroad. Where can he get hundreds. Has he got into the hands of money-lenders. He has no feeling, no heart. This I have long known: he has behaved as ill as possible for years back. This bitter truth I can no longer conceal; it is wrung from me by heart-rending agony.

Byron didn't go abroad but stayed on at university, where he spent much of his energy in crash dieting (he was prone to plumpness), boxing, gambling and sex, though he didn't seem to enjoy any of it particularly and was convinced that he would never be happy.

By the time Byron was twenty on January 22 1808, the year he was to meet Lord Grey, his debts amounted to £5,000 (£5,000,000 today). At that age he had no source of income other than what he received from his relatively impoverished mother. Instead of curbing his personal expenditure upon his majority, Byron asked Hanson to raise the rents paid by tenants who lived in cottages in Newstead's grounds. Byron also told Hanson to insist that the Newstead servants provide themselves with their own food rather than run up food bills for which Byron would be liable.

Byron was well aware that the most sensible course of action to deal with debts which by now were starting to run towards £15,000, was to sell Newstead Abbey. Except that Byron loved Newstead too much to sell it.

Instead, Byron travelled to the continent with his friend Hobhouse and four servants to escape his increasingly persistent creditors. Byron's Grand Tour, which took place in warm southern Europe countries, naturally included Greece, and it was in Greece that Byron started writing the great poem which was eventually to feature the daughter who was still almost five years from being born: *Childe Harold's Pilgrimage*.

When Byron returned to London in July 1811 he was depressed at being back in Britain and again being hard up. In addition, his mother died on August 1 1811. Resuming his life of writing poetry, being poor and borrowing, socialising and snatching such sexual opportunities as he could, he made his maiden speech in the House of Lords in February 1812 opposing the harsh Tory measures against riotous Nottingham weavers.

Then his life changed when, at the beginning of March 1812, the first two cantos of *Childe Harold's Pilgrimage* were published, soon in ten editions issued prior to the publication in 1816 of the third canto of the poem. When the fourth canto was published in 1818, by which time Ada was a toddler, the enthusiasm for the fourth canto led readers to ask that the whole poem be printed together as a single book. There is a reliable estimate that between 15,000 and 20,000 copies were printed.

Byron, as he recalled in his memoirs, had awoken one morning and had found himself famous. It fanned his love life considerably. Soon he found himself – not entirely of his own volition – involved in a liaison with the passionate and fairly eccentric aristocrat and novelist Lady Caroline Lamb (she famously remarked of Byron that he was 'mad, bad and dangerous to know'). After their liaison collapsed, he began a relationship with Lady Oxford, who was a patron on the reform movement and about fourteen years older than Byron.

Meanwhile, Byron appears to have entered into a sexual relationship with his half sister Augusta, then married to a Colonel George Leigh, too. There remained, however, the small problem of Byron's debts. While there is no doubt that his publisher, John Murray, earned a small fortune, Byron seems to have thought it vulgar to take money for his poetry. On at least one occasion, Byron asked his publisher, John Murray, to give away 1,000 guineas which Byron was owed as royalties for his poems (a guinea was one pound and one shilling, and was often used as the currency in genteel transactions). This sum, 1,000 guineas, was a vast amount indeed. What he needed rather more than another lover was a rich wife: Annabella Milbanke, for example.

$\mathcal{A}$nnabella
Anglo-Saxon Attitudes

Annabella Milbanke (she was christened Anne Isabella but was generally called Annabella) was the daughter of a wealthy family that dwelt at Seaham Hall in the small town of Seaham, about fifteen miles south of Newcastle-upon-Tyne on the coast of North-East England. Annabella was born on May 17 1792 and so she was about three years and eight months younger than Byron.

Annabella doesn't appear to have been a great beauty; she had an excellent figure but a rather snub face with pronounced, apple-like cheeks. While her considerable intelligence cannot be doubted, by nature she was reserved, pedantic and not especially good company. She was an only child and when she was born her mother was over forty. Her parents doted on her and gave her full encouragement to think highly of herself and her opinions. Up in the provincial north of England, Annabella was a proud and wealthy fish in a small pond, but when she ventured down to London she encountered many women who were more beautiful, wittier and considerably more sexually forthcoming than she was.

On Sunday March 15 1812, Annabella was down from Seaham for her second London season. The 'season' was the period, usually from the spring to late summer, when eligible young women from wealthy families – the women were known as debutantes – spent time in London's social scene, meeting new people and, hopefully, a prospective husband. The importance of the season had evolved in the seventeenth and eighteenth centuries, and peaked in its traditional form in the early twentieth century. It was once usual for debutantes to be presented to the monarch as part of their season.

That Sunday, March 15, Annabella wrote in her journal of a dinner she had with her relatives, the Melbournes. As she said: 'Julius Caesar, Lord Byron's new poem, and politics were the principal themes in conversation.'

By March 24 Annabella had read the first two cantos of *Childe Harold's Pilgrimage*. Her praise of it in her journal was not – predictably, if you knew Annabella – unqualified. She conceded that Byron excelled in the 'delineation of deep feeling, and in reflections relative to human nature' but she also wrote that he was too much of a mannerist: a word she emphasised in her journal.

It never seems to have occurred to her that her analysis might be irrelevant to the chaotic and impulsively emotional way in which he lived his life.

The first time she set eyes on him was at a waltzing party given by Lady Caroline Lamb on Wednesday March 25 1812. Unlike Ada much later, Annabella found the whole experience of being in London, and in the company of eminent and famous people, intoxicating. By now Byron was a celebrity, one of the most famous men in England. Annabella gave Byron close attention. She was naïve for her years, understandable perhaps when her parents were quite old and when her upbringing had been sheltered and she had had no siblings. It's difficult not to conclude that she simply didn't realise that Lady Caroline and Byron were having an affair. Instead what she saw, as she later wrote, was a man in 'desolate situation', surrounded by unworthy admirers and friends who didn't care for him.

Annabella (Anna Isabella) Milbanke, 1814.

Annabella's father was already wealthy, but was also the heir to an even greater fortune that could reasonably be expected to come to Annabella after his death. There's no doubt that Annabella, the intelligent but awkward, judgmental and naïve wallflower, was extremely (albeit temporarily) attractive to Byron.

Annabella confided to her journal her own thoughts on meeting him:

I saw Lord Byron for the first time. His mouth continually betrays the acrimony of his spirit. I should judge him sincere and independent – sincere at least in society as far as he can be, while dissimulating the violence of his scorn. He very often hides his mouth with his hand when speaking.

Annabella thought she had found a mind that matched her own:

It appeared to me that he tried to control his natural sarcasm and vehemence as much as he could, in order not to offend, but at times his lips thickened with disdain and his eyes rolled impatiently.

Annabella and Byron became friends, sort of. It's not entirely clear how, but she was getting better known socially, and Byron got to know her. That he felt any sudden intense attraction for her seems unlikely. Inasmuch as posterity can ever know how Byron felt at any moment of his life, his initial feelings for Annabella appear to have been a mixture of boredom and gloominess, though mingled with a flickering curiosity over whether at some point he might be able to get her into bed.

Annabella seems to have continued to be oblivious to the fact that the literary hero she found so fascinating was having an affair with Lady Caroline Lamb, and Lady Caroline and Byron didn't take any steps to disabuse her of this illusion. Except that in the summer of 1812, Caroline sent Annabella a drunken letter warning her against 'fallen angels who are ever too happy to twine themselves round the young Saplings they can reach.'

The letter very likely influenced her to reject a half-hearted marriage proposal Byron made to her in October 1812, by letter. It was a bizarre marriage proposal as Byron was close friends with Annabella's aunt Lady Melbourne, and together they delighted in gossip about Annabella's pedantry and moral rectitude. Lady Melbourne was cut from a different cloth. During her own heyday, she had been notorious for her liberal granting of sexual favours to a wide range of aristocrats: one of them was rumoured to have bought her off another for £13,000. She had had numerous children born in wedlock, but by different aristocrats. Though one of the most well-known and influential society hostesses of the period, she was fifteen years older than Byron's mother and theirs was a libertine friendship that remained pure.

Back in Seaham, on a lonely Sunday, August 22 1813, however, Annabella was staying with her parents and was obviously missing the excitement of London and her conquest of sorts; Lord Byron, the man whose name had been on everyone's lips. She sought to resuscitate her friendship with him by letter after sounding out her aunt, Lady Melbourne. After the failed marriage proposal and presumably declaration of his love, she appeared unsure of their relationship and the letter has no salutation, though it is signed formally 'Yours faithfully, A. Milbanke'.

You have remarked the serenity of my countenance, but mine is not the serenity of one who is a stranger to care, nor are the prospects of my future years untroubled. It is my nature to feel long, deeply and secretly, and the strangest affections of my heart are without hope. I disclose to you what I conceal even from those who have most claim to my confidence because it will be the surest basis of that unreserved friendship which I wish to establish between us – because you will not reject my admirations as the result of cold calculation when you know that I *can* suffer as you have suffered.

With little to do in Seaham and hearing fresh news about him, she laid out an ambitious plan for Byron's well-being:

No longer suffer yourself to be the slave of the moment, nor trust your noble impulses to the chances of life. Have an object that will permanently occupy your feelings and exercise your reason. Be good.
    Feel benevolence and you will inspire it. You *will* do good.

Annabella's letter to Byron started a strange correspondence in which they deepened their intimacy without actually meeting, rather like two people who meet on an internet dating site.

For Annabella, who delighted in writing critical accounts of people in Seaham, the medium of correspondence was perfect. She could continue to put into practice her theory about Byron – that he was misunderstood by most people and was really a sensitive and admirable person who would respond to the doting love of a cautious and prudent individual such as her.

As 1813 progressed into the autumn, Annabella began to fancy herself in love. In early October 1813 she sent her aunt Lady Melbourne (with whom she warily 'felt little sympathy' in summer) her reactions to Byron's poem *The Giaour*.

The description of Love almost makes *me* in love. Certainly he excels in the language of passion… I consider his acquaintance as so desirable that I would risk being called a Flirt for the sake of enjoying it, provided I may do so without detriment to myself – for you know that his welfare has been as much the object of my consideration as if it were connected with his own.

Byron, at this time, was writing at Augusta's home at the small village of Six Mile Bottom near Newmarket in Cambridgeshire. In response to Lady Melbourne's attempts to caution him against an affair with Augusta, Byron wrote to Lady Melbourne that he thought the risk he ran was 'worth while', but said 'I can't tell you why – and it is *not* an 'Ape' and if it is – that must be my fault.' What exactly he meant by Ape is not clear; he might have meant the common idea that the child of incest would be an ape.

Nonetheless, on November 10 1813 Byron wrote to her that he was writing another poem, also set in Turkey, and that he would like to send her a copy. This poem was *The Bride of Abydos*. In the same letter he enquired when she was likely to be in town, and flirtatiously added; 'I imagine I am about to add to your thousand and one pretendants', adding 'I have taken exquisite care to prevent the possibility of that'. While Annabelle remained on the short list, on March 22, Byron nonetheless noted in his journal that he might marry Lady Charlotte Leveson Gower, apparently because (as Byron put it) 'she is a friend of Augusta, and whatever she loves, I can't help liking.'

Fanned by Lady Melbourne – who no doubt had also provided Byron with an informed view of Annabella's financial future – Annabella was now deeply in love. 'Pray write to me,' she begged him on June 19 1814, 'for I have been rendered uneasy by your long silence, & you cannot wish me so.' And on August 6 1814, Annabella wrote coquettishly to Byron to question whether he should come to Seaham as there might be a danger that he felt 'more than friendship' towards her.

All this time, Byron had continued wooing Lady Charlotte Leveson Gower, his main prospect – marrying rather than writing for gain being the more noble pursuit. But in a major setback, on September 8 or 9 1814, Lady Charlotte wrote to Byron to tell him that her family had other plans for her romantically.

Byron, confronted with this news, panicked. 'I could not exist without some object of attachment,' he often acknowledged during this time and scrambled to get one and decided it would be Annabella. He showed the draft of his proposal to Augusta, who said: 'Well, this is a very pretty letter; it is a pity it shall not go. I never read a prettier one. 'Then it *shall* go,' said Byron.

Annabella, overjoyed, accepted at once. Byron, busy with literary business and with telling his friends about his forthcoming marriage, was in no hurry, however, to visit his prospective wife.

It was only when Annabella wrote to him on October 22 1814 to tell him that a wealthy childless uncle of hers, Lord Wentworth, had journeyed some three days to the Milbanke home at Seaham from Leicestershire expressly to meet Byron and had been most disappointed not to find him there. She added 'It is odd that my task should be to pacify the old ones, and teach *them* patience. They are growing quite ungovernable, and I must have your assistance to manage them.'

On the way to his betrothed, Byron stopped off to see Augusta and her husband Colonel Leigh who was staying with his wife, as he sometimes did. The colonel was not at all happy to learn of Byron's impending marriage, as the colonel had hoped Augusta would be Byron's only heir.

There was a more welcoming reception at Seaham. Byron was buoyed by his meeting with Lord Wentworth, who had announced he now intended to make

Annabella his heiress by his will. Then there was Annabella's family who said they would be providing a dowry of £20,000 (£18 million). This would be immediate help to alleviate his debts, which had mounted to a monumental £30,000 at the time (£28 million).

On the morning of his wedding, Monday, January 2 1815, Byron awoke in gloomy spirits, but with a determination to go ahead with the deed. By eleven o'clock in the morning Byron and Annabella were man and wife. At Six Mile Bottom, at that very hour when Augusta knew the vows would have been completed, she felt, as she put it, 'as the sea trembles when the earth quakes'.

'*Had* Lady Byron on the sofa before dinner,' Byron laconically reported on his marriage day in his memoirs which were partly remembered by various friends who had seen some of the memoirs prior to their destruction.

The newly-wed couple had arranged to spend the first few days of their wedded bliss at a Yorkshire country house, Halnaby, that belonged to the Milbanke family. Arriving at Halnaby, the ground was covered in deep snow. The servants and tenants of the Milbankes were waiting in the wintry weather to greet Annabella and Byron. A reliable source testifies that when the carriage stopped, Byron at once jumped out and walked away, not bothering to help Lady Byron down from the carriage.

As to Annabella's demeanour on arrival at Halnaby; there is conflicting evidence about this. An old butler who was there among the welcoming party remembered that Annabella came up the steps of Halnaby alone 'with a countenance and frame agonized and listless with evident horror and despair'.

A maid who had accompanied them on the journey, however, recalled her mistress as being as 'buoyant and cheerful as a bride can be.' In any event, that very same night, Annabella later recalled, Byron enquired 'with an appearance of aversion, if I meant to sleep in the same bed with him.' He often complained to Annabella, during the marriage, 'it's done,' 'it's too late now', and, 'it cannot be undone'.

Byron grew a little calmer as the weeks wore on, but when living with Annabella he was always prone to terrible moods. Byron took Annabella to Six Mile Bottom and introduced her to Augusta. It was torture. Byron and Augusta often left Annabella alone, even all night, and sometimes Byron even taunted his wife that he and Augusta had 'no need' of her.

He liked to play off the women against each other. For example, on one occasion, according to Annabella's testimony for a Deed of Separation from her husband, he threatened to 'work them both well' and lay himself down on the sofa, then ordered them to take it in turns to embrace him, while he made comparisons between them in gross language.

Strangely when Annabella finally suspected that her husband was having sexual relations with Augusta as well as with her, Annabella didn't blame Augusta, telling herself (and, eventually, others) that Augusta submitted to Byron, but that Augusta was not gratified by his affection. Some biographers have even suggested that

Annabella and Augusta had lesbian feelings for each other, for which there is no unassailable evidence.

Augusta, during the rest of her life, wrote Annabella hundreds of letters; Augusta was always weirdly fascinated by Annabella, and although Annabella didn't reciprocate as keenly, she still had a great fondness for Byron's half-sister. There were even some times of affection between Byron and Annabella. During one of these episodes in March 1815, or possibly late February, Ada was conceived.

Annabella, Lady Byron, painted during her marriage (Charles Hayter).

In April 1815 the Byrons settled in London, in a house on 13 Piccadilly Terrace which they could not remotely afford, even though Lord Wentworth conveniently died on 17 April. From now on regular harassment by bailiffs and other creditors became part of their married life.

In the persisting absence of the dowry (estates such as her uncle's took years to settle before funds would become available; it would take about a decade), Byron remained fearsomely in debt. While Byron and Annabella still managed to find time for occasional moments of passion and togetherness – Byron and Annabella both added her mother's family name 'Noel' as a double-barrel to theirs upon the death of her uncle –, these moments were snatched more and more in the face of stress caused by debts, Byron's emotional instability, and his sexual infidelity.

On Sunday December 10 1815, at 1 pm, Annabella gave birth to a girl, Augusta Ada, though soon Annabella preferred to call her only 'Ada'.

Byron and Annabella had decided Augusta would be godmother. The very fact that Annabella agreed to this (she was not the kind of woman to be coerced into something so major) suggests that her sympathies for, and perhaps liking for, Augusta, were strong.

When Byron was shown his healthy new-born daughter, he reputedly said, 'Oh! What an instrument of torture I have acquired in you!'

Annabella had by now decided that her husband had been her own instrument of torture for long enough. But she kept her intentions carefully secret, and on the night of Sunday January 14 1816, she went to bed with Byron as usual.

Early in the morning, Annabella wrapped herself and her month-old baby daughter up warmly. Without waking her husband, she stole out of their London house with baby Ada in the company of a maidservant and into a carriage that would take the three of them away from Byron and to Annabella's parents.

Byron would never see his wife, or Ada, again.

$\mathscr{T}$he $\mathscr{M}$anor of $\mathscr{P}$arallelograms

Ada's early life was spent in the public spotlight of a scandalised and titillated Britain, though her mother did her utmost to keep her out of its glare. To some extent, Lady Byron (as it seems appropriate to call her now, as she was known by this name to most of the world) was successful in this quest, though Ada was never truly out of the public's mind.

Lady Byron had left the strange, wayward, selfish and fundamentally unhappy man she had mistakenly married. And now she found herself in a life she had never planned. Her entire upbringing and attitude to life had been focused on her at some point becoming a wife and a mother.

Lady Byron went to be with her parents in Leicestershire, who at that time were staying at a country house in the village of Kirkby Mallory. Strange to say, despite her having left Byron, for a few weeks the still-married couple exchanged fond letters with each other. Byron seems to have expected that Annabella would soon return to him with Ada.

And maybe that would have happened. But after a few weeks, during which Lady Byron had been reticent with her parents about why she had left Byron, there came a time – it's not known when exactly this happened, but it would have been most likely some time in February 1816 – she told her parents about what had happened and just how Byron had behaved towards her. Her parents were furious and slowly turned her against him. She also received a note from Byron's former lover, Lady Caroline Lamb, who proposed a meeting with Annabella.

At this meeting, Lady Caroline told Annabella that Byron had committed incest with Augusta. Lady Caroline, not known for mincing her words, convinced Annabella of the truth, if she still needed convincing after the peculiar cohabitation arrangement at Six Mile Bottom. After Lady Caroline's visit it was also clear beyond doubt that Augusta and Byron's incest with each other had become widely known and discussed, and beyond the borders of Britain as well as within them. Even worse, Lady Caroline told Lady Byron that Byron had indulged in homosexual acts while at Harrow.

There was only one respectable answer, and soon Lady Byron launched a legal suit against Byron for an official separation. As for Byron, he had the last laugh, in his poem *Don Juan* – written in *ottava rima* pentameters, whereas *Childe Harolde's Pilgrimage* had been written in Spenserian stanzas – with Donna Inez.

Her favourite science was the mathematical,
Her noblest virtue was her magnanimity;

Her wit (she sometimes tried at wit) was attic all,
Her serious sayings darken'd to sublimity;
In short, in all things she was fairly what I call
A prodigy – her morning dress was dimity [a sturdy curtain fabric]…

By now desperate for cash after flunking the marriage option, Byron knew he had to sell his ancestral home in Nottinghamshire, Newstead Abbey to settle debts and for his living expenses abroad. But in fact Newstead was not sold until December 1817, when Byron was fortunate to get the colossal sum of £94,000 (today £94 million) for it from a Colonel Thomas Wildman, a wealthy military officer who had been a classmate of Byron's at Harrow. Though his financial worries were much reduced (they were never completely resolved), it would be unfair to Byron, though, to say that he forgot about Ada once abroad. During the eight years between his departure from England (he never returned) and his death, he frequently wrote to Augusta to ask her to ask Lady Byron for particulars about Ada, such as her upbringing, the colour of her hair, and so on. But he had no contact with her, or thoughts about her upbringing.

Lady Byron was adamant that Ada would be prudently educated. Most adults in the early nineteenth century regarded children as incomplete, ungrateful, savage adults – a view that Ada's friend Charles Dickens would later challenge in his writings. Children were dressed like miniature versions of adults and children's literature – such as it was – was meant for moral guidance. Lady Byron agreed whole-heartedly and was not going to sit by idly or let Ada mix much with other children who hadn't been vetted. As a result, most of Ada's childhood was rather lonely and spent in the company of older and not always congenial people.

Ada's education started when she was only four years old. It was about as comprehensive as was feasible at the time. Not easy to please, Lady Byron was prone to firing the tutors and governesses that she recruited when she considered that they were not sufficiently helpful to Ada's education. When there were extended breaks between tutors due to Lady Byron being unable to find one she considered suitable for her daughter, Lady Byron taught Ada herself.

In 1824, at the age of eight, a typical day for Ada looked like this:

Music	10
French reading	11:15
Arithmetic	11:30
Work	1:30
Music	3:15
French exercise	4:30

Lady Byron imposed a strict discipline on Ada, who altogether was rather like the only girl in a school. Through a ticket-based system Ada was either given a reward or punishment. When Ada performed well, she had paper 'tickets' bestowed on her, but these tickets got confiscated when Ada did not meet Lady Byron's expectations.

On the occasion that the ticket system failed to motivate her, she was placed in a closet until she promised to behave herself and work hard at her studies. Woronzow Greig, a mathematical and pedantic friend of Ada's when she was an adult, recounted that Ada 'acquired a feeling of dread towards her mother that continued until the day of her death', Ada's death that is.

Lady Byron, whom Byron once nicknamed the 'princess of parallelograms', was particularly keen for Ada to have a mathematical education. Lady Byron wanted to suppress Ada's imagination – which Lady Byron saw as dangerous and potentially destructive and coming from the Byrons – and wanted to make Ada, as far as feasible, completely rational.

For Lady Byron, Ada was a constant reminder of her marriage and the failure of her life's purpose. Ada, after all, was half Byron by blood, and it's difficult to conclude other than that Lady Byron frequently found her irritating and even treacherous whenever Ada was behaving in a way that made her seem too much of a Byron. She had a particularly deep mistrust of Ada's imaginative approach to science and Ada's tendency to seek playful uses for science and mathematics.

Unlike Lord Byron's savage nature, Ada's was to be chained and guided towards goodness in the way she had laid out in her fateful letter to him after she had rejected his marriage proposal.

It meant, specifically, that Ada had to be very grateful for corrections she received from adults. As Ada herself wrote on September 7 1824:

I should wish that... you do not give me reward because I think the reward of your being pleased with me sufficient[,] besides when you do that I don't do the good thing because I know I ought to do it but because I want to obtain the reward, and not because I know it to be right, and if I was encouraged in this, when I was grown up I should be a very disagreeable creature, and I should never do any good without I had a reward.

Ada wrote many such letters as, over time, Lady Byron grew into a woman extremely preoccupied with her health, and prone to following the strangest theories about good health. She was often away at various rest cures, which involved her doing such things as taking the waters in spa towns, and spending time with her aristocrat-ic friends.

On other occasions, Ada was to keep Lady Byron informed with reports that were pleasing to her and showed that she understood the purpose of her upbringing. Thus, on Wednesday May 31 1826, ten-year-old Ada castigated vanity in a letter to her mother, who was staying on the sea in Hastings, in a place called Library House. She added: 'I think it is well for me I am not beautiful.'

The next day she wrote again to keep her mother informed on what had occurred that day.

Library House, Hastings
1st June Thursday 1826
My dearest Mammy
No letter from Lady Tarn yet. Louisa [a visiting friend presumably] is a little better today. She was very much pleased yesterday with a box of the most beautiful things imaginable from Miss Noel. There were beautiful little wee wee baskets, one larger basket, and some pincushions in the form of little guitars, another carriage and Louisa is to have a dozen more carriages of different sorts.

Today I have been doing some Italian, and I have written about Arrowroot, and made out a little alphabetical list of all the things I am going to write about from *Bingley's Useful Knowledge* there are two dozen different things I wish to write about, and I have been puzzling hard at a sum in the rule of three which I could not do, the question is if 750 men are allowed 22500 rations of bread per month how many rations will a garrison of 1200 men require?

I think by the time you come back I may have learnt something about decimals, I attempted the double rule of three but I could not understand it, however I will not give it up yet, the book does not teach as well as you do... My purse is getting on beautifully. It is for Louisa's trade and though it is a coarse purple one, I have some thoughts of buying it and giving it to you.

Mrs Montgomery is very kind to me, and I am not *very* unhappy though of course I should be happier if you were here... I get up between six and half past six, breakfast at nine, dine at one, and sup at six. I hope I am not very troublesome... My watch is very useful to me here, I only wish I could wear it.... Have you got me a governess yet? ...

I must now conclude. If you have too much to do, pray don't write to me at all, I am dying to ride over on horseback to Battle to meet you on Wednesday. I wish above every thing that such an arrangement would be made.
Goodbye, yours affectionately
A. Ada Byron.

Likewise before, in her letter of September 7 1824, she reported her entire day to her mother:

My dear Mama. I got my fryed fish yesterday. Frank goes today, but he is still Gobblebook for he is reading Captain Hall. I have got a great deal of cold. How is Lady Tamworth. I hope she liked the needlebook.... Puff is on the sofa in the drawing room. I am ne[t]ting a purse. I am very sorry Flora is not here for I miss her more than ever.

The letter writing was carefully guided as well. For example, not all 1824-1826 letters (none before that date are known to exist) in the Lovelace-Byron collection at the Bodleian are in Ada's own handwriting. Several are in the handwriting of one of her governesses presumably, and they frequently start with 'Dear Annabella'. But even when the letter is in Ada's handwriting (as indeed the 'fryed fish' letter is above) there are sometimes sentences that Ada's governess either dictated to her or perhaps helped her to write by suggesting phrases.

What did Ada ask her mother about Byron? Throughout her life she herself seems always to have thought highly of him and to have wished she could see him. But the letters of her youth provide no clue. There is evidence, however, that Lady Byron simply made her father a taboo subject at home. For example, it is known that when Ada was a little girl she asked her mother whether a father and a grandfather were the same. When she asked this question – hardly a wicked one – she was severely rebuked by her mother.

As for Byron himself, despite his inconsistency in emotional matters, he does not indeed appear ever to have stopped caring about Ada and loving her in the way that seemed to suit him best – that is, from a distance. In a letter from Venice to his publisher John Murray on February 2 1818, when she was two, he wrote:

I have a great love for little Ada, and I look forward to her as the pillar of my old age, should I ever reach that desolate period, which I hope not.

A year later he writes on June 7 1819 from Bologna:

I have not heard of my little Ada, the Electra of my Mycenæ, but there will be a day of reckoning, even should I not live to see it.

He clearly hadn't forgiven Annabella for the failed dowry and marriage and the forced sale of his beloved home Newstead Abbey. Electra plotted revenge (with her brother) against their mother, Clytemnestra, for the murder of their father, King Agamemnon, leader of the Greeks in the Trojan War.

Whether Byron would have been King Agammnon to Ada's Electra is another matter, at least if his illegitimate daughter Allegra was anything to go by. Allegra was born a little over a year after Ada on Sunday January 12 1817. She was the result of a brief affair between Byron and Claire Clairmont, the stepsister of Mary Shelley, wife of the poet Percy Bysshe Shelley.

Allegra was born in the town of Bath, in England as 'Alba', and when she was a baby lived with her mother and the Shelleys. However, when Allegra was fifteen months old, Claire gave her to Byron. Claire was under serious financial pressure and the Shelleys did not want Allegra to live with them. Nor did Byron's half-sister Augusta. So Claire journeyed to Italy to give the baby girl to the baby's father, who had asked Claire to baptise the child 'Allegra Byron'. Byron himself even discussed changing the spelling of Allegra's surname to 'Biron'.

Allegra didn't live with Byron either, but with a succession of people Byron paid to look after her. But she did visit him on occasion. He wrote approvingly to a friend, 'My bastard came three days ago… healthy, noisy and capricious.'

Byron liked the physical resemblance between Allegra and himself, but he hardly spent any time with her, and she only ever learned Venetian Italian, not English, because she was brought up by paid Venetian carers. In March 1820, he complained that Allegra was 'obstinate as a mule' and at the age of four, Allegra frequently had temper tantrums in front of Byron. She was packed off to be in the care of the nuns at the Capuchin convent in Bagnacavallo. They looked after her well, but in 1822, at the age of five, the little girl died, either of typhus or malaria.

Despite seeing Annabella as Clytemnestra, Byron continued to write to her about Ada. In 1820 he sent a locket with his hair for his five-year-old daughter to carry around with her (it seems unlikely that Annabella was in a hurry to pass this on to Ada), and received a portrait of Ada in return.

Augusta Ada Byron.
from a miniature

Ada Byron, after a miniature.

Just before his death he asked for 'some account of Ada's disposition, habits, studies, moral tendencies, and temper, as well as her personal appearance.' Annabella wrote back:

> Her prevailing characteristic is cheerfulness and good temper. Observation. Not devoid of imagination, but is chiefly exercised in connection with her mechanical ingenuity – the manufacture of ships, boats, etc… Tall and robust.

And so Ada, like Allegra, grew up remote from Byron both geographically and emotionally – unaware of her father's warm interest in her. She was frequently ill as a child; her health was never particularly good and suffered from headaches and all manners of other childhood ailments. When Ada was seven and a half, she became particularly sick. She suffered from an illness that gave her especially sharp headaches, and even affected her eyesight in such a way that her doctor ordered her education to be halted. Lord Byron heard about her illness in 1823, not long after arriving in Greece to help the Greeks fight to win their freedom from the Ottoman Empire.

He was so upset about hearing of Ada's illness that he stopped writing in his journal, and his peace of mind about Ada was only to some extent restored when Lady Byron wrote to him in early 1824, saying that Ada felt better.

This correspondence between Byron and his wife was usually carried out via Augusta, with whom Byron was in regular contact, but sometimes Lady Byron wrote to her estranged husband directly.

Byron's life on the Continent had been his usual round of affairs with both sexes, along with travel and writing poetry. But he had eventually found robust and reliable passionate love with a young Italian countess, Teresa Guiccioli, who was small and voluptuous, and who had auburn curls. She also reportedly had large and luminous eyes, a fresh, youthful face and a large bust that some thought was so out of proportion with her figure that it made her look dumpy.

After Byron told Teresa he was leaving for Greece she pleaded with her poet lover to let her accompany him, but he refused. Bored, the romantic idea of helping to free the Greeks from the Ottoman Empire was his new grand passion. Soon after arriving in Missolonghi, Byron became ill with flu, which developed into a more severe fever.

He died on Monday April 19 1824, cursing his doctors, although according to the account of his valet, the last words Byron actually spoke were: 'Oh, my poor dear child! – my dear Ada! my God, could I have seen her! Give her my blessing… '

An enormous crowd viewed his funeral entourage, which consisted of forty-seven carriages passing through the streets of London. His body lay in state for two days in London, on July 9 and 10 1824.

Byron's friends led a campaign for him to be buried in Westminster Abbey in Poet's Corner, as a tribute to the quality of his work. But these calls did not find favour and, instead, Byron, who had travelled so far both geographically and emotionally in his life, was buried only about six miles from his ancestral home of

Newstead Abbey, in the Byron family vault at the church of St Mary Magdalen in a Nottingham village called Hucknall.

Neither Lady Byron nor Ada attended the funeral. Ada did know of it, however, for her September 7 1824 'fryed fish 'letter above was edged in black in memory of the death of her father.

George Noel Byron, the poet, had been the sixth Lord Byron. The poet's cousin, a naval officer called George Anson Byron, inherited the baronetcy and became the seventh Lord Byron.

This new Lord Byron became a good friend of Lady Byron, presumably because there was no further need for estrangement after Byron's death. And George went with his family – taking along with him his own son and heir, yet another George, who was only eighteen months younger than Ada – to visit Lady Byron and Ada.

Clearly Lady Byron was keen for the vacuum of 'Lord Byron' to be filled, and to encourage Ada's idea of kinship. On September 13 1824, Ada wrote to George, a cousin several times removed, calling him her 'dearest brother', an affectionate letter whose ideas no doubt came from the adults around her.

> My dearest brother, for so my love I can justly call you. I have been considering what a great misfortune it is for me not to have brothers and Sisters but I look upon you as one that I can talk to as a brother or a Sister... and when you die, I shall have none that are so well suited to my age to talk to... If ever you come to settle with me for some time how happy will my time be... I can then show my affection and love in a thousand ways, your death would therefore be to me a very severe blow of grief...

Mentioning her visit to the Hercules that had sailed her father to his death, she added

> I went to see papa's ship and liked it very much but I should have liked it better if my brother George had been there...

She had never met the boy, but these words no doubt helped pave the way to rapid normalisation of family relations, expunging the unpleasant ructions of the past.

5

The Art of Flying

In her early years of bringing Ada up, Lady Byron received financial help from her family. But in 1825, a great financial year for Lady Byron, she got the abundant sums of money she needed to live as she wanted to live and to bring Ada up in the style she wished to raise her daughter.

By 1825, Lady Byron's mother had died and she had inherited money from her. Lord Wentworth had passed away in 1815, and finally the funds, too, had become available, a decade later. Combined with her inheritance from her mother, she was now a very wealthy woman. Her days of poverty with Byron were over. He had taken his debts with him in his grave. She now owned estates in Leicestershire that provided a substantial income.

Lady Byron now also owned coal mines in the north of England, and lived in luxury with Ada on the proceeds of the coal mined from them and from her rents. Meanwhile, of course, the coal-miners lived from hand to mouth in damp, cold cottages. Lady Byron, though, often sponsored schemes to help educate her miners' and tenants' children.

For Lady Byron, it was a great adventure to educate Ada. The little girl was famous throughout the nation because of her father, and Lady Byron was aware that her education of Ada would itself soon come under the spotlight.

As Ada passed from girlhood to womanhood, Lady Byron's educational energy, far from flagging, increased.

The usual educational opportunities open to girls in the early nineteenth century varied from limited to non-existent. Even middle-class and aristocratic girls were usually only taught such skills as were necessary for overseeing the management of the households they could one day expect to oversee.

Many professional educators, even female ones, actually believed women's minds to be inferior to men's at a fundamental biological level. The fallacious reason often given at the time was that women's brains are on average smaller in physical mass than those of men.

Lady Byron's zeal as an educator stemmed from the unusually broad education she had herself received as the only daughter of wealthy, liberal, forward-thinking parents. She had studied history, poetry, literature, French, Italian, Latin, Greek, drawing and dancing. Lady Byron was was now rich enough, and confident enough, to get what she wanted.

That, of course, did not mean that Ada would find an outlet for her mental energies after her education was completed anymore than Lady Byron had done herself.

Even for a girl of Ada's socially elevated class who yearned to lead a mentally fulfilling life, opportunities were close to non-existent. There was generally little alternative but to marry, produce children and live for one's husband. The idea of Ada doing anything other than marry would not have entered her mother's mind. Ada's education was there to stock her mind. Beating a path for science, however, was anathema. Lady Byron, to whom Ada was in thrall for much of her life, was conscious of how disastrous her own marriage had been. She was determined that Ada would marry an aristocrat who could offer Ada a secure, comfortable domestic life. Ideally, Lady Byron wanted Ada to marry into the *older* aristocracy as there was a particular appeal at the time for titles that were more than a century old – indeed, such as the Byron baronetcy.

Lady Byron, now rich, influential and strong-willed, was quickly getting – if she wasn't already – used to having her wishes obeyed. Ada's yearning to lead a life of the mind, readily expressed even in the letters she wrote as a teenage girl, was thus doomed from the start. She was destined to spend much of her life aching to use her mind, but was confronted with the day-to-day reality of children, nannies, servants, running a household and dealing with a husband's whims.

Some middle-class women, such as Jane Austen, the Brontës or – later in the century – George Eliot won careers for themselves through successful authorship. When they did, the reality of their struggle was likely to be a key subject of their books; Charlotte Brontë's *Jane Eyre* (1847), for example, is largely autobiographical in its account of the predicament of an intellectually gifted young woman forced to confront the rigid limitations of life as a governess.

It was also true that, occasionally, enormous talent along with a stroke of good fortune, might give a woman an opportunity to escape the bonds of domesticity. Another middle-class woman, Mary Somerville, later a close friend of Lady Byron and Ada, who was to achieve international renown as a mathematician and scientist and was to have the first Oxford College for women named after her in 1879, had first became interested in mathematics when she amused herself by solving the often challenging mathematical puzzles that were frequently published in Victorian embroidery magazines.

Not an inch of such freedom beckoned in Lady Byron's grand designs for her aristocratic daughter.

Instead in June 1826, ten-year-old Ada embarked with her mother and her governess, Miss Stamp, for the Continent. They travelled with a range of friends and one of Lady Byron's cousins, a Robert Noel.

Annabella hadn't dared take Ada abroad while Byron was still alive. Byron had been desperate to see Ada, and Annabella feared he might hear of his daughter's arrival on the Continent and try to have her kidnapped. In style, they made a fifteen-month Grand Tour of the continent.

Ada loved the sensory explosion that touring brought to her quiet life. On one occasion she wrote to the Scottish poet and dramatist Joanna Baillie, a friend of Lady Byron and Ada, how beautiful she thought the Alps were, and how she could see them from every street in the Turin. At the time, Turin was the capital of the kingdom of Sardinia, and a prosperous city of more than 150,000 inhabitants, splendidly sited on the rapid-flowing Po river with great views of the Alps. The city reappears in our story in due course because, as chance would have it, it was there that a mathematician called Charles Babbage found a more interested and committed audience than he was readily able to find in Britain.

Ada enjoyed sketching as well as writing, and she drew some chalk sketches of the Alpine scenery in Switzerland. She also wrote about being impressed by the steam boats she saw on Lake Lucerne, and how she enjoyed the organ music she had heard in the churches. At one point she even speculated that she might make a career as a singer. Ada was given to developing passions. When learning the violin as a child, she did so while walking around the billiard table as she was so absorbed in her studies that it was feared that she would otherwise not get enough healthy exercise.

Mary Somerville, 1834 (Thomas Phillips).

In the autumn of 1827, Lady Byron and the eleven-year-old Ada were heading back with Ada's governess, Miss Stamp, from their fifteen-month grand tour of Continental Europe.

After their return to England, Lady Byron rented Bifrons, the imposing country house at Patrixbourne, Kent, that was a day's coach-drive from London and far enough to be secluded, and moved there with her daughter. Life resumed its usual pattern and for much of the early part of 1828, Lady Byron was away visiting friends or at various 'rest cures', leaving Ada alone with her governess, her various tutors, and her beloved cat, Puff, one of whose kittens she promised to her 'brother' George, the heir of the new Lord Byron.

With her mother often away, Ada now relied somewhat on Puff for emotional support. She wrote in French from Bifrons, on her twelfth birthday, December 10 1827, all about him to a lady called Flore, presumably her French tutor.

> This morning Madame Puff gave me a pretty gift of a purse, which she presented to me in the most gracious manner between her two fore-paws, the truth is that Miss Stamp had the kindness to make the purse, and then made Madame Puff give it to me, and it is quite a curious thing enough that while Miss Stamp was making this purse, Puff jumped onto her lap every so often and watched the work or pushed her nose against the silk as if she were taking an interest in it.
> Goodbye,
> Your affectionate
> AAB

With little else providing interest at Bifrons, what happens in Puff's life makes a frequent appearance, too, in Ada's letters to her absent mother.

> Your grand-daughter [Puff] has taken up all her kittens into a very nasty dirty hole in the roof of the house where nobody can get at them, she stays with them all day long & only comes down for her meals. I suppose their bed is made of cobwebs, and I think that Puff cannot have a very refined taste.

And on January 8 1828:

> My dear Mammy… Puff is a naughty cat and has got a little hiding place in the chimney of my room where she puts the birds she catches and there she leaves them till she is hungry and wishes to eat one, this morning she took one of them under my bed and gave me the satisfaction of hearing her crunch each bone as she eats the bird.

It was still only months after the exciting year and a half on the road through Europe; in the same letter about her cat crunching a bird's bones, she hit on the daydream of flying:

> I wish that supposing I fly well by the time you come back you would, if you are satisfied with my performance, present me with a crown of laurels, but it must only be on condition that I *fly* tolerably well. Pray do not ask me whether

I get on well or ill with my flying because as I mentioned before you went I do not wish you to know anything about it till you come home and even then I shall only let you know by my actions…
Your affectionate young Turkey…

Ada grew more and more interested in the idea of flying. No longer were hers just idle daydreams of a teenager. Ada's had an unmistakable structure and purpose to them: she wasn't only interested in the idea of flying, she passionately wanted to build a flying machine. She was deeply fascinated by the practical challenges of the task, and thought out its practicalities during her solitary, writing to her mother, still her only confidant, on Wednesday April 2 1828.

Since last night I have been thinking more about the flying, & I can find no difficulty in the motion or distension of the wings, I have already thought of a way of fixing them on to the shoulders and I think that they might perhaps be made of oil silk and if that does not answer I must try what I can do with feathers.

I know you will laugh at what I am going to say but I am going to take the exact patterns of a bird's wing in proportion to the size of its body and then I am immediately going to set about making a pair of paper wings of exactly the same size as the bird's in proportion to my size.…

I ought not to forget to tell you that in my new flying plan, if it answers, I shall be able to guide myself in the air by a method I have lately thought of. I have now a great favour to ask of you which is to try and procure me some book which will make me thoroughly understand the anatomy of a bird, and if you can get one with plates to illustrate the descriptions I should be very glad because I have no inclination whatever to dissect even a bird. I do not think that without plates, I could be made thoroughly to understand the anatomy of a bird.…

Five days later Ada wrote another letter, again to her mother, about her plans. By now Ada's speculations had progressed to the dream of powered flight.

As soon as I have got flying to perfection, I have got a scheme about a… steamengine which, if ever I effect it, will be more wonderful than either steampackets or steamcarriages. It is to make a thing in the form of a horse with a steamengine in the inside so contrived as to move an immense pair of wings, fixed on the outside of the horse, in such a manner as to carry it up into the air while a person sits on its back. This last scheme probably has infinitely more difficulties and obstacles in its way than my scheme for flying, but still I should think that it is possible…

The day after writing this letter, Ada wrote to Lady Byron again, though now Ada had evidently been chastened by a letter from her mother indicating Lady Byron's disapproval of the thinking-time she was giving to her pioneering of aviation.

My dearest Mammy. I received your letter this morning & really do not think that I often think of the wings when I ought to think of other things, but it was very kind of you to make the remark to me....

I have now decided upon making much smaller wings than I before intended, and they will be perfectly well proportioned in every respect, exactly on the same plan and of the same shape as a bird's. Though they will not be nearly enough to try and fly with, yet they will be quite enough so, to enable one to explain perfectly to any one my project for flying, and will serve as a model for my future real wings.

It wasn't the first time Ada and her mother would disagree over the nature and direction of Ada's interests, and it wouldn't be the last. Ada's fascination with flying continued and on Wednesday April 9 1828, she wrote to Lady Byron:

... great pleasure today in looking at the wing of a dead crow and I still think that I shall manage to fly and I have thought of three different ways of flying that all strike me as likely to answer.

It was not much later that Lady Byron hired a tutor at £300 a year to teach Ada mathematics. It equates to around £225,000 today and it was a small fortune. Clearly Lady Byron thought her daughter merited such an expensive education, and she wrote to him with careful instructions:

There are no weeds in her mind; it has to be planted. Her greatest defect is want of order, which mathematics will remedy. She has taught herself part of Paisley's Geometry [presumably Batty Langley's *Practical Geometry* 1726, dedicated to Lord Paisley], which she liked particularly.

Despite everything, in this respect it seems that Lady and Lord Byron were in complete agreement who their grown-up daughter should be. When Byron had asked from Greece for a description of his daughter's character just before his death, he had added:

I hope the Gods have made her anything save poetical – it is enough to have one such fool in the family.

$\mathscr{L}$ove

When in 1837 Benjamin Disraeli, a novelist before he became one of Britain's most famous politicians, based the heroine of one of his novels closely on Ada, such was Ada's celebrity due to the fame of her father's separation from her mother that he could take it for granted readers would recognise his portrait of her. Disraeli named the Ada character 'Venetia' – the eponymous name of the novel – and the Lady Byron character 'Annabel', with only a slight change of spelling of the original.

Having begun his novel in traditional nineteenth-century style, with a lengthy description of the ancient, ivy-draped country house, Cherbury, in which the drama, such as it is, takes place, Disraeli continues:

> This picturesque and secluded abode was the residence of Lady Annabel Herbert and her daughter, the young and beautiful Venetia, a child, at the time when our history commences, of very tender age. It was nearly seven years since Lady Annabel and her infant daughter had sought the retired shades of Cherbury, which they had never since quitted. They lived alone and for each other, the mother educated her child, and the child interested her mother by her affectionate disposition, the development of a mind of no ordinary promise, and a sort of captivating grace and charming playfulness of temper, which were extremely delightful.

As far as is known, Disraeli never met either Ada or Lady Byron. Nonetheless, Disraeli's romantic take no doubt reflected the views of the chattering classes of the time, who'd all read Byron's lampoon of his wife:

> Lady Annabel rose from her seat, and walked up and down the room, speaking with an excitement very unusual with her.
>
> 'To have all the soft secrets of your life revealed to the coarse wonder of the gloating multitude; to find yourself the object of the world's curiosity, still worse, their pity, their sympathy; to have the sacred conduct of your hearth canvassed in every circle, and be the grand subject of the pros and cons of every paltry journal, ah, Venetia! you know not, you cannot understand, and it is impossible you can comprehend, the bitterness of such a lot.'

If that wasn't purple enough, Disraeli continued with gusto his baroque relief of a wronged woman pining for death to release her from her heartache.

'I have schooled my mind,' continued Lady Annabel, still pacing the room with agitated steps; 'I have disciplined my emotions; I have felt at my heart the constant, the undying pang, and yet I have smiled, that you might be happy. But I can struggle against my fate no longer. No longer can I suffer my unparalleled, yes, my unjust doom. What have I done to merit these afflictions? Now, then, let me struggle no more; let me die!'

Lady Byron, though, had no intention of dying as a result of the year she had spent with Byron. There was far more sport in enjoying her money and rest cures. Nonetheless, Disraeli's novel does suggest that Lady Byron had a point when she picked remote places for Ada to reach maturity. Far removed from fashionablesociety and its gossip, there was no risk that anyone would cause Ada to be upset, or ask questions, by referring to the shadows of the past.

Ada turned thirteen on December 10 1828 and entered a new phase of her life. Her governess Miss Stamp, whom she liked so much, was leaving the employ of Lady Byron at the end of 1828. Instead of hiring another governess, Lady Byron decided, for the time being at least, to make use of various of her friends to develop Ada's mind, enhance her studies, and exercise a good moral influence over Ada.

Then, early in 1829, Ada became very ill. She was bedridden until the middle of 1832. The illness had a profound effect on Ada and she lost her dreamlike insouciance and gained focus. She continued her studies with great ardour for the three years when she was bedridden. Lady Byron took care to ensure that Ada did not try to do more than her health permitted, but she now worked hard and was frequently very tough on herself and her educational failings, even though Ada precociously mastered German on her own.

If ever Ada came close to being Lady Byron's aristocratic mini-me, it was now. Ada reports on occasion that she has gone for a few turns in her wheelchair, and the tone she adopts towards her studies and herself is often indeed serious and even self-chastening. On occasion she is even not adverse to making sneaky comments about her mother.

To her cousin Robert Noel, who had joined their Grand Tour, Ada writes in flawless German.

27 August 1830

I thank you for your letter, and especially for your beautiful handwriting. I am reading Schiller's translation of Macbeth which I find very interesting because I have never read the play in English. Maybe when I have [read] this work I can obtain one of the books you have so kindly recommended. Miss Doyle and I are reading German together and like the lame and the blind we assist each other.

Her recovery was painfully slow, however. Barely able to move or write, she had lost her appetite for activities such as riding or imagined ones such as flying.

I don't think you would recognise me, that is how much I have changed since you saw me; I am getting stronger step by step, and with the help of crutches I can go for walks. I lost my taste completely for riding and flying and such, but I feel well enough to play a little piano which give me great pleasure, and if you would be so kind to send me some light pieces of German music, I would be very happy. I especially like the waltz. I hope to hear from you again, even though I cannot write a letter twice as long as you would like me to. Miss Doyle sends her best regards and I do also, my dear cousin.

A. Ada Byron

The next part of Ada's upbringing is chronicled by a particularly fascinating document, a short biography of Ada (written in about 1847, the precise date is not known) by Woronzow Greig.

Ada had got to know her future biographer when she and her mother moved to Fordhook Manor in 1832. She was now sixteen, overweight from having been bedridden for three years, but the time was rapidly approaching when she would be expected to enter London society and find an aristocratic husband. It was time for the oyster shells of her childhood to open and filter in the outside world.

Fordhook was in Ealing, today, a suburb of London. But at the time when Ada and Lady Byron lived at Fordhook, Ealing was a separate village, located about eight miles west of the centre of London, and popular with wealthy people who wanted to escape the smells and bustle of the capital, yet remain within easy access to London.

It was – possibly unintended by Lady Byron – a witty literary choice that might have amused libertine Lord Byron. One of the manor's claims to fame was that it had been the home of the writer Henry Fielding (1707-1754), the creator of immortal, wordy but entertaining and somewhat bawdy novels such *Joseph Andrews* (1742) and *Tom Jones* (1749). These novels were written some decades before the 1830s, when the drawbridge of middle-class morality had come down and started greatly inhibiting what could be said in respectable print about sex. It was not until the last decade of the nineteenth century that writers again dared pushed the boundaries of what was acceptable, such as Thomas Hardy, with his sensuous novel *Jude the Obscure* (1895), though its furore led Hardy to abandon novel-writing.

Lady Byron gave Ada more leeway at Fordhook than Bifrons but recruited three friends no less to help supervise Ada's education and demeanour. Ada referred to the three women as the 'Three Furies' and, resenting their presence in her life deeply, she did all she could to escape their influence. Her success rate was low. Greig wrote 'As Ada grew older the interference of these ladies became more insufferable, but every attempt to resist it was [illegible] by Lady Byron.'

Born in 1805 and ten years older than Ada, Greig was the son of Mary Somerville. Ada and Lady Byron got to know Mary through Dr William Frend, a by that time ancient Cambridge mathematician who had been Annabella's tutor when she was young, and whom she had recruited to teach Ada mathematics, too. (Frend was no stranger to avant-garde thinking; a convert to Unitarianism, he had taught his daughter Sophia Hebrew and philosophy, and been one of the tutors of the influential economist Robert Malthus.)

Born on December 26 1780 as daughter of Captain (later Vice-Admiral) William Fairfax, Greig's mother Mary Somerville was another female genius, a Scottish science writer and polymath, who mastered mathematics, astronomy and other sciences later in life.

Mary had been brought up in Scotland with her brother who was three years older than she was. A sister was born when Mary was seven, and a second brother when she was ten. The two brothers were given a good education but, in keeping with the ideas of the time, little need was seen to educate girls so Mary's parents provided virtually no education for their daughter.

As a young child what little education she did receive was from her mother, who taught her to read but didn't consider it necessary to teach her to write. When Mary was ten years old she was sent to a Miss Primrose's boarding school for girls in Musselburgh (a few miles east of Edinburgh on the Firth of Forth) but only because her father considered her somewhat of a brute. The school in Musselburgh neither gave Mary a happy time nor a good education. She spent only one year there and, on leaving, felt (in her own words) 'like a wild animal escaped out of a cage'.

After this Mary returned to her home and began to educate herself by reading every book that she could find in her home. Far from encouraging Mary in her voracious reading, members of her family such as her aunt criticised her for spending time on this unladylike occupation. In order that she might learn the correct skills for a young lady, Mary was sent to a school in Burntisland where she was taught needlework.

However, one member of Mary's family did encourage her educational ambitions. When visiting her uncle in Jedburgh near the English border Mary told him that she had been teaching herself Latin. Far from being cross, her uncle encouraged her and the two would read Latin before breakfast while Mary stayed with him in Jedburgh.

When Mary was about thirteen, the family rented a house in Edinburgh where they spent the winter months, the summers being spent in Burntisland. Mary balanced her life between the social life expected of a young lady at this time and her own private study. She did learn many skills that were seen appropriate for a young lady. In addition to the needlework, she learnt to play the piano and was given lessons in painting from the artist Alexander Nasmyth, then in his thirties, an outspoken supporter of the French Revolution and friend of the famous Scottish poet Robert Burns.

Ada Lovelace (née Noel Byron), 1832.

In fact it was through Nasmyth that Mary first became interested in mathematics. She overheard him explaining to another pupil that Euclid's *Elements* formed the basis for understanding perspective in painting, but much more, it was the basis for understanding astronomy and other sciences. This comment inspired Mary to study Euclid.

There was another quite different reason why Mary became interested in studying algebra. She read an article on the subject in a woman's magazine belonging to a friend. Her younger brother's tutor was able to provide Mary with algebra texts and help introduce her to the subject. Mary became so engrossed in mathematics that her parents worried that her health would suffer because of the long hours of study that she put in, usually during the night. Her father believed (not uncommon at the time) that 'the strain of abstract thought would injure the tender female frame'.

In 1804, when Mary was twenty-four years old, she married a distant cousin, Captain Samuel Greig. Mary and Greig went to London but Mary found that her husband did not understand her desire to learn. As she put it, 'he had a very low opinion of the capacity of my sex, and had neither knowledge of, nor interest in, science of any kind.'

Samuel Greig died three years after the marriage. By this time Mary had given birth to two sons – one was Woronzow Greig – and on the death of her husband she returned to Scotland with them. She now had a circle of friends who strongly encouraged her in her studies of mathematics and science.

In particular John Playfair, then professor of natural philosophy at Edinburgh, encouraged her and through him she began a correspondence with a former pupil of Playfair called William Wallace. In this correspondence they discussed the mathematical problems set in the *Mathematical Repository* and in 1811 Mary received a silver medal for her solution to one of these problems. At this time Mary read, among other things, Sir Isaac Newton's famous *Principia* (1687).

In 1812 Mary Greig married William Somerville, an inspector of hospitals. William was the son of her aunt Martha and her husband Thomas Somerville in whose house she had been born.

Unlike her first husband, William was interested in science and also supportive of his wife's desire to study. By the time Ada and Lady Byron met Mary, she was well on her way to becoming not only one of the greatest female mathematicians in the world, but one of the greatest mathematicians of either sex.

Indeed, she soon proved to be one of the most remarkable intellects of the nineteenth century. Her book *Connection of the Physical Sciences* became famous.

Her son Woronzow soon became a close friend of Ada as well as, later, her lawyer. It is quite clear that, like all of London society, he was fascinated by Ada, and had a romantic interest in her. The feeling wasn't reciprocated, but she enjoyed shocking him and he lapped up her shocks eagerly and faithfully.

His biographical document about Ada is in seven foolscap handwritten pages. Unfortunately, most of the document is illegible; legible handwriting was not regarded as necessary for a gentleman in the early nineteenth century and Greig was a determined gentleman. The biography is often illegible at precisely the moment when it is most interesting.

My first recollection of Ada Byron about 1832 or 3 is when as a young girl she was a visitor at the house of my mother at the Royal College Chelsea. She was very intimate with Mrs [illegible] who was about her age and as she had even in those early years a decided taste for science which was much approved by Lady Noel Byron [Annabella]....

Greig continues with an almost photographic glimpse of the teenage Ada:

She used to lie a great deal in a horizontal position, and she was subject of fits of giddiness, especially when she looked down from any height. As might be expected at this early passage of her life, she had not much conversation. She was reserved and shy, with a good deal of pride and not a little selfishness which developed itself with her advancing years. Her moral courage was remarkable and her determination of character most pronounced.

Greig's pages are particularly interesting because Ada completely trusted her lawyer's discretion, and gave him an unobscured view of her life:

In afterlife I became very intimate with her; quite as much so as it is possible for persons of different sexes to become consistently with honour. Her communications to me were most unreserved.

From Greig, then, we learn of Ada's first love-affair and how she successfully escaped the suffocating shackles of the three furies to be with her first lover, a young tutor.

A short time before my family became acquainted with Lady Byron and her daughter... the services of a young man, the son of John Hamble... to come for a few hours daily to assist her daughter's studies.... tenderness soon sprang up between these young people. This was not observed... by Lady B and the three furies.

Ada had no intention for their love affair to remain pure, and things moved almost to the point of a full 'connection':

.... managed to place in the young man's hands a scrap of paper appointing an assignation at midnight in one of the outhouses [of Fordhook]. The assignation took place and Ada informed me that matters went as far as they possibly could without connection being completed. After this Ada's feelings towards the young man naturally became stronger and more uncontrollable.

The formidable Lady Byron got wind of the friendship, but clearly didn't have the full measure of what had happened, and soon Ada dramatically and impetuously eloped.

At length the mother's eyes were opened and the young man's visits were discontinued. Driven to madness by disappointment and indignation at the conduct of the furies… Ada fled from her mother's house to the arms of her lover who was residing at no great distance with his relatives, Lady B's friends.

Ada, when a younger girl, once made the mistake of remarking what a beautiful voice she had. 'Ada,' Lady Byron responded sharply, 'do you think you gave yourself your voice?' There can be little doubt that Lady Byron knew exactly what to do to rein in her daughter and collect her from her hugely-embarrassed friends. A guilt trip is a modern term, but, if Ada's letter of March 8 1833 is anything to go by, that was unmistakenly her lot.

Fordhook
My dear Mama. I must now thank you for your last very kind letter. Though deeply impressed by the ceremony I attended on Sunday for the first & I hope not the last time, certainly I had no inclination to weep. – The more I see & the more I think & reflect, the more convinced do I feel that no person can ever be happy who has not deep religious feeling and does not let that feeling be his guide in all the circumstances of life. Had I entertained my present sentiments two years ago, I should have been now a very different person from what I am. But I am yet quite yet in the spring of life & hardly indeed full blown. I trust I may be spared many years longer, & may thus be allowed the opportunity of showing that *I am an altered person.*

Slightly feebly, Ada includes in the same letter a barb to Lady Byron about the lapse of a mother's power to oblige her daughter.

If you said to me, 'do not open the window in my room,' I am bound to obey you whether I be 5 or 50. But if you said to me, 'don't open your room window. I don't choose you should have your window open,' I consider your only claim to my obedience to be that given *by law*, and that you have no *natural* right to expect it after childhood. The one case concerns *you & your* comfort, the other concerns *me only* and cannot affect or signify to you. Do you see the line of distinction that I draw? I have given the most familiar possible illustration, because I wish to be as clear as possible. Till 21, the law gives you a power of enforcing obedience on *all points;* but at that time I consider your power and your claim to cease on all such points as concern *me alone*, though I conceive your claim to my attention, and consideration of *your* convenience and comfort, rather to increase than diminish with years…

Four days later, however, Ada already backtracked and sent her mother a brief additional letter which contains these particularly illuminating lines:

You know I always must sermonize a little when I write to you. – I am very well, & the bones are flourishing.

7

Silken Threads

On June 5 1833, London high society consisted of barely five thousand people, many of whom were related to one another by marriage or infidelity. They had substantial capital in the bank, enjoyed the best food and drink, mostly didn't need to work, and were waited on by a small army of servants for whom servility was an essential professional skill. Leisured society was a constant round of big lunches, frenetic amorous liaisons, leisurely afternoons and glittering soirées.

The million or so people who comprised the rest of London's population, like the vast majority of Britons at the time, scraped by on a diet rarely much above starvation level, and did their best to snatch such grimy slivers of happiness and scraps of life as they could.

Fashionable society's London was the comparatively small area of the capital that stretched southwards from Marylebone Road in the north to the River Thames in the south. Charles Babbage, the mathematician who was to become very important in Ada's life, lived at number one Dorset Street, near Manchester Square, and dwelled only a few hundred yards inside that unmarked but comprehensively recognised northern boundary.

The aristocracy and the ordinary people were like different species. A commoner might rarely be elevated to nobility by acquiring great wealth or political influence, but the easiest way into the aristocracy – then as now – was through marriage. Most aristocrats married other ones, but occasionally a commoner might get lucky, just as sometimes happens today.

Many aristocrats had gained their fortune by inheritances that usually dated back to land taken by the invading Normans after 1066 from Britain's Anglo-Saxons.

Three decades into the nineteenth century, social conventions of British life seemed, on the surface, to be stronger than ever. But in truth Britain was changing fast. One of the biggest causes of change was the enormous impact of machine technology that so fascinated Ada. In 1829, the Scottish essayist and historian Thomas Carlyle had written an essay that, by 1833, was famous. The essay, 'Signs of the Times', elaborated on how Carlyle thought the epoch in which he found himself should be seen:

Were we required to characterise this age of ours by any single epithet, we should be tempted to call it, not an Heroical, Devotional, Philosophical, or Moral Age, but, above all others, the Mechanical Age. It is the Age of Machinery, in every outward and inward sense of that word; the age which, with its whole undivided might, forwards, teaches and practises the great art of adapting means to ends. … On every hand, the living artisan is driven from his workshop, to make room for a speedier, inanimate one. The shuttle drops from the fingers of the weaver, and falls into iron fingers that ply it faster… For all earthly, and for some unearthly purposes, we have machines and mechanic furtherances…. We remove mountains, and make seas our smooth highways; nothing can resist us. We war with rude Nature; and, by our resistless engines, come off always victorious, and loaded with spoils.

In 1833, few would have disagreed with any of this, least of all Ada or her future friend Charles Babbage. Yet Carlyle could have said even more. It was not only that the machinery revolution was changing how goods were made and how things were done. Even more importantly, the revolution also helped to liberate people's imaginations about how things *might* be done, and allowed creative thinkers to speculate on exciting possibilities for using one type of new mechanical technology in conjunction with another, or with several others, to imagine new uses that were not yet technologically possible. This was precisely the kind of thinking in which Ada excelled; indeed, she was arguably one of the most innovative thinkers in this respect of her epoch.

As for the spirits of self-analysis and self-appreciation that had so thoroughly infused Carlyle's essay, these were rife in a Britain that had emerged in 1815 from twenty years of war with France as the world's richest economy, its military hegemon, and its self-appointed leader.

The man who had ruled this confident and energetic land since June 1830 was King William IV, the former Duke of Clarence, third son of the famously mad King George III. William, sixty-seven years old in 1833, was an avuncular, self-deprecating, rather comic, silvery-haired fellow, and the oldest person ever to have ascended the British throne. His record still stands today.

The Prime Minister was Lord Grey. His Whig party had convincingly won the first General Election held after the broadening of the electorate, the creation of new constituencies to accommodate the burgeoning urban middle-classes, and the scrapping of tiny, barely-inhabited constituencies known, appropriately enough, as 'rotten boroughs' following the passage in 1832 of the Reform Act.

Throughout the nineteenth century, the fraction of the British population entitled to vote had grown more and more awkwardly at odds with how Britain was developing as a rapidly urbanising nation. In 1831, for example, just 4,500 people in Scotland out of a total of 2.6 million people were entitled to vote. In Britain in its entirety – which in the 1831 Census was recorded as having a population of 13.1 million – the electorate was only about three percent of adult males.

But even after the passage of the Reform Act, there was a wealth qualification attached to the right to vote and the vast majority of men were still excluded from voting by it. Women were regarded as inherently undeserving of the suffrage.

Princess Victoria, the daughter of William IV's younger brother, was the heir to the throne and looked set to become queen before long, but women were otherwise dismissed in political life. Ada would never have Babbage's opportunities in a world where women were regarded as providers of pleasure and babies.

With the 1832 Reform Act on the Statute Book, Britain's ruling class felt the danger of revolution to be past. Those with money and health could relax; this was a good time to be British.

The British domestic economy had been growing fast over the past few decades, fuelled by the demands of the increasingly prosperous and populous middle class who wanted good clothes, quality furniture, fine cutlery and excellent ornaments. Yet what had really made Britain the world's richest country was the immense success of British exports. No other country in the world controlled such vast overseas markets.

The expanding British Empire played a hugely important role in Britain's surging prosperity. It was the largest the world had ever seen – the Roman Empire had been quite small by comparison – and the British Empire was still growing. By 1833, as well as including the entire British Isles (Ireland was part of Britain then), the empire already consisted of Canada, India, New South Wales, Jamaica, British Honduras, Malta, the Ionian Islands, Bermuda, Trinidad, British Guiana, Gibraltar, Gambia, Sierra Leone, the Cape colony at the southern tip of Africa, various other small possessions and, in the Far East, Penang and Malacca.

The empire was the overseas legacy of the same British spirits of adventure and inventiveness that had caused so many changes back home. In the 1830s, the British liked to see it as having a reforming and civilising influence, governing people who were supposedly not fit to govern themselves. But at heart the Empire was a vast, efficient machine for making money for Britain, and the same Britons who liked to preach the Christian virtues had little compunction about plundering property, land and other wealth from the peoples they governed.

At home, the British textile industry was enjoying particularly phenomenal growth. It had hardly featured in the export figures back in 1750, yet by 1833 about one-half of all British exports were textiles. The expansion of the textile industry needed the coal and iron industries, and these three industries all forged forward in a dynamic symbiosis. Coal was powering the steam-engines that operated much of the machinery used in making textiles, while iron was used to build the machinery itself and was an important building material of the manu-factories that housed it. Water power was still important, but the British towns that had expanded the most were the ones located near the coal-fields, especially the vast reserves in the north-east of England.

Britain's war with 'rude nature' that Carlyle observed was, in particular, sustained by the success of its textile industry. New textile industry machinery had played and was still playing the leading role in the growth of the British economy.

About a century earlier, in May 1733, an ingenious inventor, John Kay, was granted a patent for his 'flying shuttle'. This did not actually fly, but involved the shuttle being shot through a loom along wheels in a track. The weaver pulled a cord to operate the flying shuttle. Kay's invention speeded up the weaving process enormously, dramatically increasingly yarn consumption, so much so that the flying shuttle spurred the invention of new machines that would spin yarn from cleaned and combed wool more rapidly than ever before.

The invention in 1764 by James Hargreaves of the spinning jenny (named after his daughter) was the first major breakthrough in textile machinery that comprehensively met this new challenge. The spinning jenny greatly increased the rate at which yarn could be spun, though the thread produced by Hargreaves's machine was coarse and lacked strength, making it suitable only for use as weft: that is, the threads woven at right angles across a warp when making fabric.

In 1771, Richard Arkwright, a former barber who had become interested in textiles while carrying on a sideline as a wig-maker, patented his 'water frame' which produced a yarn of a superior quality to that yielded by the spinning jenny. Arkwright built factories employing hundreds of people.

In 1779, Samuel Crompton's 'spinning mule' or 'mule jenny' combined the main benefit of the water frame (the quality of its yarn) with the speed of the spinning jenny. Ever since about 1790 most of the yarn-spinning machines in Britain had been Crompton's mules. Meanwhile, Edward Cartwright in 1784 had invented the first steam-powered loom. By 1833, almost all the garments produced in Britain were woven on powered looms.

In 1833, the motive ingredient of all new discoveries was considered to be steam power. Charles Babbage yearned to build a calculating machine driven by steam; a teenage Ada imagined a steam-powered flying-machine. Steam power was the wonder of the age, offering the ability to get machines to work more quickly and much more reliably than the traditional sources – man, horses and water.

The inventor who had made steam truly the motive force of the British Industrial Revolution was James Watt, a Scottish instrument-maker. He hadn't invented the first steam engine: that honour went to Thomas Savery, who patented a cumbersome steam pump in 1698. But Watt's engines were easily the best. His successful endeavour to correct the inefficiencies of earlier machines had attracted the attention of Matthew Boulton, a Birmingham-based industrialist who manufactured decorative items and engaged Watt to build him a steam-engine.

Boulton, a sort of brusque self-parody of what industrialists were supposed to be like and frequently were like, quickly grasped that steam engine manufacture could itself be a highly successful commercial venture. In 1775 Watt and Boulton had gone into business together. Their collaboration made Watt rich and Boulton richer still. By 1800, Boulton and Watt's factory in Birmingham had produced more than 500 steam engines. Boulton liked to take influential guests around his factory, boasting that he sold 'what every man desires: POWER.'

In 1833, factories throughout Britain were equipped with their own rotary steam-engines, whose revolving shafts were connected by a network of drive-wheels, belts and pulleys to dozens of individual looms, spinning mules, spindle mills and to all kinds of powered machines.

While very efficient and complicated in design, Britain's machinery was relatively plain in its purpose. The truth is that by 1833, the most sophisticated, fully operational machine ever devised was not a British invention at all. Neighbouring France – for several centuries Britain's arch-enemy but by 1833, a somewhat strained political ally – too, was having its own 'industrial revolution'. The very expression was the invention of a Frenchman, the diplomat Louis-Guillaume Otto, who on July 6 1799 had written to a friend to say that *'une revolution industrielle'* had started in France.

In 1833, the most ingenious and versatile textile machine in the world was a French silk-weaving loom developed in the early years of the nineteenth century by Joseph-Marie Jacquard, a master silk-weaver from Lyons, and patented by him in 1804. It was this machine that fascinated Ada.

The Jacquard loom was a mind-boggling invention. It was used by weavers who wanted to weave luxurious silk fabrics that featured images, such as portraits, still lifes, or even landscapes. These 'figured' fabrics were enormously popular and commanded the highest prices round the world.

The silk business in Lyons had been so successful that by the early nineteenth century, about 30,000 people in Lyons – an actual *majority* of the working population – earned their livings from silk. Brawny workmen would load heavy wrapped silk fabrics into the backs of horse-drawn carts for transportation along the two great rivers, the Rhône and the Saône, on whose convergence the city is built. Prosperous merchants lingered over their glasses of absinthe at streetside cafés, boasting to their business rivals of the latest deal they had made with wealthy customers, who might easily include a member of Europe's many royal families.

Before the Jacquard loom was introduced, figured fabrics could only be created painfully slowly (at the rate of about an inch of fabric woven per day) by two weavers. One worked the shuttle, the other (known as the 'draw-boy', though it was usually men who were employed in this role rather than boys) was perched on a platform above the loom and worked hundreds of strings to govern which warp threads should be raised and lowered for a particular woven image.

The Jacquard loom transformed this cumbersome process by allowing just one weaver to create the images automatically, using a long chain of punched cards that controlled the complex configuration of the warp threads when an image was being woven into silk. The loom's invention allowed a lone weaver to work about twenty-four times as fast as before. One weaver, equipped with a Jacquard loom, could produce around two feet of finished figured fabric every day. Everyone was happy except the draw-boys, who, reputedly, ambushed Jacquard in Lyons and tossed him into the Rhône.

By 1833, the new loom was already well known in Britain. Ada's imagination was set alight by the idea of any machine, like the Jacquard loom, that, once designed and built, could give humankind revolutionary control over processes that had previously either been impossible to control or else only in an haphazard, erratic way.

As she went out with her mother, on the evening of Wednesday June 5 1833, to a party in fashionable London, she was fated to meet that evening the one person in Britain who understood her driven interest in mechanical questions that had so exhausted her mother, a man who was driven in a way that matched her own – Charles Babbage.

As a result of their elective affinity, seventeen-year-old Ada Byron's insight into the future of calculation would erupt into a new and most radical kind of imagining, and give her a vision of a kind of Jacquard loom that wove, not silk thread, but mathematics. In other words, a Jacquard loom that operated like a computer.

8

When Ada Met Charles

We know about the first time Ada met Babbage from her mother Lady Byron's writing to a Dr William King two days later. One of Lady Byron's obsessions in bringing up Ada was that if Ada's imagination was not checked, it would cause disaster to Ada and those around her, just as Ada's father Lord Byron had done. Lady Byron believed that if Ada studied mathematics, her imagination would be rendered harmless. Lady Byron appears to have recruited King for Ada's moral improvement, especially to try to keep in check any thoughts that Lady Byron regarded as wayward.

Born in 1786, King was a British physician, philanthropist, lunatic asylum manager and devout Evangelical Christian from Brighton. He is best known today as an early supporter of the Co-operative Movement, a programme of community-wide social movements designed to bring members (usually of poor communities) the benefits of clubbing together to buy goods and services at better prices. Lady Byron maintained a lively correspondence with him on a number of subjects, and on that day wrote two pages on current medical obsessions (she was a fervent hypochondriac) and about an investment she had decided to make.

In 1833, Ada was about to turn eighteen and Lady Byron could be reasonably pleased with her daughter's progress to adulthood. On Friday May 10 1833, less than a month before Ada met Babbage, she had been presented at court, a ritual most daughters of prominent members of London society went through to mark their passage into womanhood. After her presentation at court, Ada could be invited to 'society' events and would also be regarded as marriageable to the right man, or we should perhaps say, to the right title. Lady Byron was adamant that as and when her daughter Ada married, it would be to an aristocrat, and ideally one whose nobility was at least a hundred years old, for such titles were accorded a specially elevated status among mothers of Lady Byron's calibre, determination and sense of rank.

Ada enjoyed her moments in the royal gaze. She curtsied to the king and his wife Queen Adelaide. Ada was also introduced to various foreign dignitaries who happened to be visiting the king and queen.

Lady Byron described the event in a letter to a friend:

Ada wore white satin & tulle. She was amused by seeing for the first time – the Duke of Wellington – Talleyrand [the famous then seventy-nine-year-old French diplomat] – and the Duke of Orléans [the French king's oldest son, who was five years older than Ada]. She liked the straightforwardness of the first – the second gave her the idea of an 'old monkey' – the third she thought very pleasing.

One might have thought the pomp and glamour of the royal court whose Empire straddled the world and a handsome prince would have dazzled a sheltered eighteen-year-old. But to Dr King, Lady Byron noted with obvious approval that her daughter was more impressed with meeting scientists on Wednesday June 5 1833 rather than royalty. In particular Ada greatly enjoyed meeting the forty-four-year-old Charles Babbage:

> Ada was more pleased with a party she was at on Wednesday than with any of the assemblage in the *grand monde*. She met there a few scientific people – amongst them Babbage with whom she was delighted. I think her power of enjoying such society is in a great measure owing to your kindness in conversing with and reading with her on philosophical subjects.

Babbage, as prone to exuberant enthusiasm as Ada, told mother and daughter about his Difference Machine, in effect a machine to make calculations:

> Babbage was full of animation and talked of his wonderful machine (which he is to shew us) as a child does of its plaything.

His was indeed a remarkable machine. Babbage wasn't the first inventor to try to build a machine for carrying out reliable calculation. In 1642 the French scientist and philosopher Blaise Pascal had tried to make an adding-machine to aid him in computations for his father's business accounts. The machine consisted of a train of number wheels whose positions could be observed through windows in the cover of a box that enclosed the mechanism. Numbers were entered by means of dial wheels. But Pascal's machine turned out to be unreliable and it never made any impact in mechanising calculation.

The German mathematician, Gottfried Wilhelm Leibniz, saw Pascal's machine while on a visit to Paris and worked to develop a more advanced version. Pascal's device was only able to count, whereas the instrument Leibniz developed was designed to multiply, divide, and could even extract square roots. He completed a model of the machine in 1673 and exhibited it at the Royal Society, but Leibniz's device did not work properly either and was never anything more than a curiosity.

Pascal's and Leibniz's machines differed in one vitally important respect from the device Babbage planned to make. Theirs were manual devices, but Babbage was adamant from the outset that his own calculation machine would be automatic. Unlike Pascal's and Leibniz's attempts, which required meticulous human intervention every stage of the way, the first calculation machine Babbage conceived – his Difference Engine – was designed to produce results automatically, with the operator only having to turn the handle that powered the machine. Even the handle-turning process could have been mechanised: there was indeed no reason why a small steam engine could not have been connected to the machine to do the job.

It wasn't just science enthusiasts such as Annabelle and Ada who were intrigued by Babbage. In 1832, the need for such a calculating machine was becoming urgent. The more extensive the role technology played in society, the more serious the problem of potentially inaccurate mathematical tables became.

If you were using inaccurate logarithmic tables to carry out an important calculation, your calculation was doomed from the start. Even worse, you had no way of knowing exactly where an inaccuracy in the mathematical tables might be found. John Herschel, writing in 1842 would observe: 'An undetected error in a logarithmic table is like a sunken rock at sea yet undiscovered, upon which it is impossible to say what wrecks may have taken place.' If properly designed, a mechanical calculator would side-step any human errors and as science seeped more and more into the economy, the huge potential benefits it could offer became more obvious even to those with little interest in pure mathematics.

An especially painful illustration of the problem would be seen in the work of the English mathematician William Shanks. In 1853 Shanks announced that he had successfully calculated, to an astounding total of 530 decimal places, the basic mathematical ratio. This, the ratio between the circumference of a circle and its diameter, is a special number in mathematics that begins 3.14159 and proceeds with a never-ending series of decimal places. Shanks devoted the next twenty years of his life to extending the approximation further to try to take the evaluation into new and undiscovered realms of mathematical achievement. But unfortunately for Shanks, an error in the 528th place meant that his subsequent life's work was entirely wasted. (Shanks was spared the anguish of this knowledge as the error was only discovered after his death.)

Ada and Annabelle's excitement about meeting Babbage was due to the fact that in December 1832, he, his chief engineer Joseph Clement and a team of workmen finished building the only mechanical device in the world that, in its day, challenged the Jacquard loom in complexity: the demonstration piece of his calculating machine, or the Difference Engine, as he called it, on which he had been working for the past twelve years interrupted only by the death of his wife in 1827. The demonstration piece quickly became the talk of scientific London. Babbage, who was always something of a showman, loved talking about the device to guests and putting it through its paces in front of an audience.

The carriage mechanism was and is fantastically ingenious (it is today in the Science Museum, London). It is enacted by a column of helically arranged arms, situated on each of the three tiers of wheels, that are visible at the back of the machine. These rotate during each calculation cycle and pull each of the figure wheels in turn to see if there is a carry to be taken into account from the last addition. The carriage mechanism, clearly visible at the back of the device when the demonstration piece is being operated, creates a remarkably beautiful oscillation of the helically-arranged arms, which has the appearance of endlessly changing and rippling waves.

The demonstration piece was able to carry out some calculations, though not sufficient of these to have the commercial application of the fully working Difference Engine, which Babbage knew would transform the creation of mathematical tables. The demonstration piece was built of bronze and steel and stood about two and a half feet high, two feet wide and the same amount deep. Today it still works exactly as Babbage planned. It can produce calculations for mathematical tables, and can also extract roots and undertake additions, subtractions, multiplications and divisions.

While only representing part of the Difference Engine that Babbage planned, the demonstration piece was immensely impressive. By June 1833, it resided in the drawing-room of Babbage's home, and he greatly enjoyed showing it to visitors, hence his invitation to show it to Ada and her mother, who keenly accepted.

Charles Babbage's Difference Engine.

9

The Thinking Machine

Ada and Lady Byron visited Babbage at his home at number one Dorset Street on Monday June 17 1833, just twelve days after they first met him. Babbage lived there on his own after the death, in 1827, of his beloved wife Georgiana, in childbirth.[3] He had made a desultory attempt to remarry after a year-long tour of the continent, then had thrown himself into his work and building the Difference Engine, a fiendishly expensive project even for a relatively well-off man as Babbage.

In 1823, following a desperate application by Babbage to the Government, he had originally been given a grant of £1,500. This money was awarded, as the Government put it, 'to bring to perfection a machine invented by him for the construction of numerical tables.' But it was a fraction of what was needed. The grant helped to accelerate development on the demonstration piece, but Babbage and his Joseph Clement, his chief engineer regularly quarrelled. A major reason for the tension between them was that Babbage insisted on treating Clement as a servant rather than a colleague, though it didn't help that Clement often sent Babbage invoices considerably larger than what had been agreed.

After 1827 Babbage had redoubled his efforts. The Duke of Wellington – Prime Minister from January 22 1828 to November 16 1830 and also for a little less than a month late in 1834 – had taken a personal interest and by 1833 Babbage had received about £17,500 (£60 million today) from the government as a grant to help him build the Difference Engine. This was a fabulous sum, enough to pay for two battleships, but all Babbage had to show for the money was the demonstration piece. Babbage had spent too much of the Government's grant on continually refining the design of these components. The machine required the production of several thousand cogwheels to precise specifications. It has been argued that the engineering of his day could not make cogwheels to the specification he required. This however is not true; modern research demonstrates that Babbage actually specified levels of precision that were *greater* than those he required.

In the summer of 1833, despite having built a portion of his beloved engine and being the talk of London, in truth his project was at a dead end. He was getting nowhere with his plan to build the whole machine. There was no precision metal industry in the 1820s, and so the only way of making these cogwheels was laboriously by hand, which was also extremely expensive. Besides, precise cogwheels and the other parts could only be made very slowly, and Babbage needed many thousands of cogwheels. While he was rich – his difficult father had died as well in 1827, leaving him a fortune of £100,000 – his funds were not unlimited.

So Babbage welcomed the distraction afforded by the visit of Ada and Lady

Byron's and demonstrated to them the one-seventh portion of the Difference Engine that had been built at the expense of so much money and heartache.

Lady Byron described her visit with Ada to Babbage's home in a letter she wrote to Dr King four days after the visit:

We both went to see the thinking machine (for such it seems) last Monday. It raised several Nos. to the 2nd and 3rd powers, and extracted the root of a quadratic equation. I had but faint glimpses of the principles by which it worked. Babbage said it had given him notions with respect to general laws which were never before presented to his mind. For instance, the Machine would go on counting regularly, 1, 2, 3, 4 &c to 10,000 and then pursue its calculation according to a new ratio… He said, indeed, that the exceptions which took place in the operation of his Machine, & which were not to be accounted for by any errors or derangement of structure, would follow a greater number of uniform experiences than the world has known of days & nights. There was a sublimity in the views thus opened of the ultimate results of intellectual power.

But Ada's response was different. She saw more than just the whirring, beautifully moving cogwheels of Babbage machine that brought mathematics to life in an exciting elegant way. Many years later, Sophia Frend, the daughter of Ada and Lady Byron's former mathematics tutor, claimed in her memoirs to have been present on the evening when Lady Byron and Ada saw the demonstration piece of the Difference Engine in action for the first time.

Lady Byron's contemporary correspondence with Dr King makes no reference to Sophia, or indeed to anyone else, being there except Ada, Lady Byron and Babbage. It's possible that Sophia (who says other visitors were there) had heard about the impression the Difference Engine had made on Ada the first time Ada saw it. But Sophia's remarks are worth quoting, because even if she wasn't there she would most likely have heard from a first-hand source, perhaps even from Ada or Lady Byron, just how entranced Ada was by the machine.

While other visitors gazed at the working of this beautiful instrument with the sort of expression, and I dare say the sort of feeling, that some savages are said to have shown on first seeing a looking-glass or hearing a gun… Miss Byron, young as she was, understood its working, and saw the great beauty of the invention.

Unlike her mother, she understood how Babbage's brilliant innovation linked the world of mathematics to a physical machine. At its heart, lay his decision to build his machine from cogwheels. Babbage had made this important practical decision about the technology at the heart of his planned calculation machine early on in his deliberations. Although we don't know exactly what drove his decision, it isn't difficult to guess the reasoning as it was the only technology available.

Babbage's conception of the Difference Engine was based on the idea that teeth on individual cogwheels (described as 'figure wheels' by Babbage) would stand for numbers. The machine's operation would be based around meshing independently-moving cogwheels arranged in vertical columns with each other. This meshing process would carry out an arithmetical calculation.

Babbage decided to use our familiar, everyday counting system of base 10 for his machine. This derives purely from the fact that the normal human allocation of fingers and toes is ten of each. He arranged things so that the cogwheel at the bottom of a vertical column would represent the units, the cogwheel second from the bottom the tens, the cogwheel third from the bottom the hundreds, and so on.

For example, the setting of a four-digit number such as '6,538' would require the bottom cogwheel to be turned eight teeth to represent '8': the second cogwheel from the bottom to be turned three teeth to represent '3'; the third cogwheel from the bottom to be turned five teeth to represent '5'; and the fourth figure wheel from the bottom to be turned six teeth to represent '6'. All the figure wheels above the fourth wheel would all be set to zero. The value of any number was therefore capable of being set in the machine in a vertical stack of cogwheels as long as there were enough wheels in the vertical stack to cover the tens, thousands, tens of thousands, hundreds of thousands, millions etc that were required to evaluate the calculation.

Babbage had christened his first calculating machine the Difference Engine because its entire operation was based on a mathematical concept called the 'Method of Differences'. This method was a technique for calculating mathematical tables by repeated regular additions of the 'differences' between successive items in a mathematical series. A mathematical series is a set of numbers (terms) in ordered succession, the value of each being determined by a specific relation to the preceding number. To take a simple example, the numbers 1,2,3,4,5 and so on to infinity comprise the series with a formula that requires 1 to be added to each previous number.

The beauty of the Method of Differences is that it simplifies the process of calculating a long and complex mathematical series. It allows otherwise difficult multiplications to be replaced by numerous straightforward but monotonous additions. But of course, if a machine is carrying them out, their monotony does not matter.

And the beauty of Babbage's numbered cogwheels was that they could be made to do these additions because, firstly, a cogwheel is, by definition, a gearwheel. It facilitates the meshing with another cogwheel. Secondly, and equally importantly, a cogwheel allows the transmission of energy in defined, incremental steps. It's precisely this attribute which makes cogwheels essential in 'counting time' in mechanical clocks. They are an essential part of the escapement: the device in a clock or watch that alternately checks and releases the train (i.e. the connected elements of the mechanism) by a fixed amount and transmits a periodic impulse from the spring to the balance wheel or pendulum.

Thus the machine had all the ingredients that excited Ada, here was a machine that showed how one could one day fly through mathematical formulas. Despite their many differences, not least their age, class and wealth, Ada and Babbage were fascinated by the same problems but approached them from different angles.

Babbage, like many of the intellectuals of his time, was fascinated by ideas of fate and predestination. He was also intrigued by the puzzle of how to reconcile the increasingly important influence of machines, who did what man wanted, with a belief in a God who, according to the theology adhered to by many people at the time, was supposed to look down on the human world like a sort of senior judge and intervene on occasions when he saw fit.

He was especially intrigued by their regularity and reliability and he got a deep satisfaction from watching properly calibrated ones going about their paces, their mechanism invariably reaching the same point in the cycle after precisely the same interval as the previous time. Unlike Ada, he saw machines essentially as mechanised servants of mankind rather than as a new area of discovery with its own mysteries. His scientific imagination was ultimately more prosaic and less incandescent than hers.

While gregarious like Ada, Babbage could also be singularly eccentric, and had a tendency to be gruff, morose and occasionally a show-off and know-it-all. In addition to this, he had a bizarre habit of talking about the most commonplace events as if they were mathematical phenomena. It made him a guaranteed attraction for fashionable society, who delighted in having Babbage in its midst. Hosts and hostesses were always delighted to be able to inform their prospective guests that Mr Babbage would be attending. In an age when much social chit-chat involved exchanging mere superficial pleasantries, a lunch, supper or soirée with Babbage present was certainly never boring.

One could never guess just what Babbage would say next. If the evolution of technology had been a little speedier and given television to the early nineteenth century, Babbage might easily have become a 'mad scientist' TV personality, popular on talkshows, and hired to host documentaries about technological innovations.

He had the advantage over Ada in that, as he was a man, scientists enjoyed his company, too, and respected him. In January 1832, the geologist Charles Lyell had travelled to Hendon, at that time a village north of London, and visited his friends and fellow geologists Dr William Fitton and William Conybeare.

We have had great fun in laughing at Babbage, who unconsciously jokes and reasons in high mathematics, talks of the 'algebraic equation' of such a one's character in regard to the truth of his stories etc. I remarked that the paint of

Fitton's house would not stand, on which Babbage said, 'no: painting a house outside is calculating by the index minus one,' or some such phrase, which made us stare; so that he said gravely by way of explanation, 'That is to say, I am assuming revenue to be a function.' All this without pedantry, and he bears well being well quizzed by it. He says that when the reform is carried he hopes to be secularised Bishop of Winchester. They were speculating on what we should do if we were suddenly put down on Saturn. Babbage said: 'You Mr Leudon (the clergyman there, and schoolmaster, and a scholar), would set about persuading them that some language disused in Saturn for 2,000 years was the only thing worth learning; and you, Conybeare, would try to bamboozle them into a belief that it was to their interest to feed you for doing nothing.'

Obviously relishing the memory, Lyell added:

Fitton's carriage brought us from Highwood House to within a mile of Hampstead, and then Babbage and I got out and preferred walking. Although enjoyable, yet staying up till half-past one with three such men, and the continual pelting of new ideas, was anything but a day of rest.

Like Lyell, Ada, for her part, found in Babbage a man whose mind she could engage with and who was as excited about ideas as she was. For her the demonstration piece of the Difference Engine she saw in action that Monday evening at Babbage's house wonderfully exciting. Seeing it, she felt filled with a completely new sense of purpose and direction.

From her childhood onwards, she had been torn between two opposite poles. She was conscious of being the daughter of the poet Lord Byron, Britain's most celebrated Romantic poet, a man whose memory in death loomed larger than it had in life, and of being the daughter of Lady Byron, whom her father had – according to her mother – so thoroughly wronged.

Ada's mind was circumscribed by her mother's wishes, and they had often threatened to overwhelm her own personality. But now Ada sensed the possibility that her friendship with Babbage might at some point lead to a new life of her own, a life of the mind that was hers and not that of her family's.

10

𝒦inship

The friendship between Charles Babbage and Ada Lovelace was to grow one of the great friendships of the history of science. It is possible to trace the friendship in considerable detail by means of following chronologically the extant correspondence between Babbage and Ada. This correspondence spans the years from June 10 1835 to August 12 1852, which was when Ada wrote her last (known) letter to Babbage.

The surviving correspondence between them consists of eighty-five letters from Ada to Babbage and twenty-five letters from him to her. There are often references in the correspondence to other letters that have apparently not survived. Moreover, in 1853 Babbage wrote a letter to Lady Byron's solicitor [Woronzow Greig] in which Babbage referred to an 'extensive correspondence' he had carried on with Ada 'for years'. He is surely referring to a correspondence much more extensive than what survives. Indeed, in the year 2000, a small cache of letters from Ada to Babbage turned up in the store-room of the Northumberland County Archive in the north of England. It is possible that more letters between them may yet materialise. Most of the letters that do survive date from the year 1843, the year Ada was at her most productive as a scientist.

It may well be why so many letters survive from 1843 is that, while Lady Byron destroyed most of Babbage's letters to Ada after Ada's death (or delegated the job of destruction to someone else), she felt morally obliged as a dedicated amateur mathematician to keep the letters relating to her daughter's great intellectual effort of that year.

At first, the friendship advanced relatively slowly. When Babbage and Ada met, she was still only seventeen and he a widower of forty-two. He was not a shy man but nor was he the kind of man who would have been excessively forward in developing the friendship. Had he been, there was always Lady Byron to contend with.

Ada was greatly impressed by Babbage. She regarded him with what she was to describe in a letter to her mother in late 1839 as a 'fondness…. by no means inconsiderable.' Ada and her mother kept in contact with Babbage and it seems certain Ada saw him on several other occasions as her mother's search for a suitable husband continued.

Ada was dealing with the avuncular Dr William King, whom Lady Byron had recruited to be her moral guide They went on 'pleasant walks' where he would instruct on how to control one's imagination and thoughts. She sweetly wrote him on Sunday 9 March 1834 that she was '*really* & permanently awaking to a sense of religious duty'.

Repeating to him his ideas in her words and using them slightly against him – the style of writing that dominates the letters to her mother – she tells him what will help her with 'self-government' of her imagination.

I must cease to think of living for pleasure or self gratification; and there is but one sort of excitement, if indeed it can be called by that name, which I think allowable for me at present, viz: that of study & intellectual improvement. I find that nothing but very *close & intense* application to subjects of a scientific nature now seems at all to keep my imagination from running wild, or to stop up the void which seems to be left in my mind from a want of excitement.

She asks him to improve his teaching of mathematics, the other area in which Lady Byron expected Dr King to tutor Ada, by laying out a syllabus for him to put together:

I am most thankful that this strong source of interest does seem to be supplied to me now almost providentially, & think it is a duty vigorously to use the resources thus as it were pointed out to me. If you will do me so great a favour as to give me the benefit of your advice and suggestions as to the *plan* of study most advisable for me to follow, I shall be most grateful. – I may say that I have *time* at my command, & that I am willing to take *any* trouble.

It appears to me that the first thing is to go through a course of Mathematics – that is to say – Euclid, and Arithmetic & Algebra; and as I am not entirely a beginner in these subjects, I do not anticipate any serious difficulties, particularly if I may be allowed to apply to you in any extreme case. My wish is to make myself well acquainted with Astronomy, Optics & c; but I find that I cannot study these satisfactorily for want of a thorough acquaintance with the elementary parts of Mathematics… In short, here I am ready to be directed! I really want some hard work for a certain number of hours every day…
Yours most gratefully & affectionately
A A Byron

Like Mary Somerville, a year after meeting Babbage, Ada's sharp mind had found a subject to focus on – and a burning passion for mathematics had awoken within her.

11

*M*ad *S*cientist

Babbage was born some three years after Lord Byron on December 26 1791 in Walworth, Surrey, nowadays Elephant and Castle in London, after the coaching inn with that name. His father, Benjamin Babbage, himself born in 1753, was a wealthy goldsmith and banker. The two professions were then closely linked; it was a small step for customers who were buying gold and jewellery from their goldsmith to use the safes in goldsmith's offices to store all their valuables and for the goldsmith to advance money on his clients' valuables.

The Babbages had been well established since the late seventeenth century in Totnes, a small town in the county of Devon in the south-west of England, about 220 miles from London.

Today Totnes is a busy little market town, especially popular with people living New Age and alternative lifestyles. Its population, about 8,000 now, has not greatly increased since the end of the eighteenth century, when it was extremely wealthy by the standards of the day.

The historical prosperity of Totnes originated from wool sheared from the backs of the sheep that spent much of their lives in the meadows on the hills that ripple around the town. This wool was turned into an inexpensive, coarse, long-lasting woollen cloth called kersey. There was a huge demand for this cloth throughout Britain and abroad for workmen's breeches and trousers.

Benjamin Babbage gradually built up his activities in the town and the surrounding district. He didn't open a bank, but traded more informally, lending out sums, transacting business under his own name, and acting an agent for some London banks. Business was brisk. Benjamin was an astute businessman.

By the start of the 1790s, the Totnes cloth trade was visibly waning. Machines powered by steam were making an impact on weaving and all aspects of fabric-making. The new form of power provided what seemed at the time to be close to unlimited energy. The steam engine also offered the enormous advantage that it was no longer necessary for mills and factories to be located near running water for operating water-wheels. Coal was the fuel of the future, and in this new industrial world Totnes was at a big disadvantage, for Devon had, as far as was known, no large natural endowment of coal. The Industrial Revolution was gathering momentum and Totnes was being left behind.

A canny fellow, Benjamin was quick to spot the significance of the new developments. He decided to transfer his business activities to London, a radical move indeed in those days, when the vast majority of the population lived out their lives in the village or town where they were born. It has been said that many people who lived in villages in the days before significant urbanisation never met more than about seventy-five other people in their entire lives, and in a town like Totnes the number would have been higher.

Benjamin moved to London in 1791, taking with him his wife, Elizabeth, whom he had married the year before. He had first-class business contacts in the capital and eventually became a partner of Praeds Bank in London, probably one of the banks for which he had acted on an agency basis.

Benjamin had always made his own luck, and there was really nothing accidental about his success in London. He chose to move to the great capital – then the largest city in the world – at a time when there was a huge increase in the demand for credit, mainly caused by the burgeoning Industrial Revolution. The banking business was literally a golden opportunity for lenders who could keep their heads and had the skill to distinguish good credit risks from bad. Benjamin possessed that skill. He prospered.

The only surviving portrait of Benjamin shows a man with a rather jovial expression (money may have been on his mind), and the look of having a precise understanding of his importance in the world and his success. Little else, however, is known about his personality except what can be inferred from the letters about him written by his son Charles and Charles's wife Georgiana.

Judging from the letters, Benjamin was frequently prone to moods that were anything but jovial, at least in how he treated his eldest son. Benjamin was often impatient with Charles and frequently even abusive to him, accusing him of failing to make serious career plans for the future, even initially refusing to approve his wish to marry Georgiana until he had made safe headway in some suitable recognised profession.

Georgiana came from a family of quality, had a fortune of her own and was by all accounts a thoroughly charming and good person. But Benjamin, a self-made man, believed that young men should make money a higher priority than matrimony, like he had.

On Benjamin's death in 1827, Charles inherited almost his entire fortune, including Benjamin's cash in the bank and his silver and gold plate, was worth about £100,000. To set this amount in perspective, when Charles Dickens died in 1870 after a lifetime of working harder than almost any writer has ever worked – overwork undoubtedly contributed to his early death – he left £98,000 in his will.

How much would Babbage's £100,000 be worth today? A reasonable rule of thumb is that for the first seventy years or so of the nineteenth century (when there was little price inflation), sums of money should be multiplied by about fifty times to give an approximate idea of what they would be worth today. However, in practice, due to the poverty of the vast majority of people, which meant that food, drink and domestic service were even cheaper than the 'fifty times' ratio, between modern prices and prices from 1800 to 1870 implies, a multiplier of about 200 makes more sense. On that comparative scale, £100,000 would be equivalent to around £20,000,000 today. (Relative to income per capita now and then, today's equivalent would be £113 million; or yet higher, £300 million, if its share of GDP is taken into account.) This figure is a more accurate estimate of Babbage's net worth than the £5,000,000 would be. Benjamin's legacy freed his son from financial care for the rest of his life and made possible the liberation of Charles Babbage's scientific imagination and to follow any pursuit which interested him.

What is known about Babbage's childhood comes from his autobiography, *Passages from the Life of a Philosopher*, published in 1864 when he was seventy-two. Babbage liked to think of himself a philosopher rather than a mathematician or man of science. (The term 'scientist' did not become current until the 1890s.)

The son of a business man, Babbage was destined for a good education. When a boy of eight or nine, he was sent by his father to a small school in Alphington, a village then a mile and a half from the city of Exeter on the south side. Apart from his time at this school, and some time he spent at the King Edward VI Grammar School in Totnes, young Charles was mostly educated by tutors, though he also attended an academy at Enfield. There, under the inspirational tutelage of the Reverend Stephen Freeman, he 'imbibed' Freeman's great love of mathematics.

As Babbage writes in his autobiography, among the books at the Enfield school

was a treatise on Algebra, called 'Ward's Young Mathematician's Guide.' I was always partial to my arithmetical lessons, but this book attracted my particular attention. After I had been at this school for about a twelvemonth, I proposed to one of my school-fellows, who was of a studious habit, that we should get up every morning at three o'clock, light a fire in the schoolroom, and work until five or half-past five. We accomplished this pretty regularly for several months.

Quite unlike Byron, he was always a well-behaved child and recalls how he lost his nurse at the age of five, while walking across London Bridge looking at ships.

My mother had always impressed upon me the necessity of great caution in passing any street-crossing: I went on, therefore, quietly until I reached Tooley Street, where I remained watching the passing vehicles in order to find a safe opportunity of crossing that very busy street.

In the meantime the nurse, having lost one of her charges, had gone to the crier, who proceeded immediately to call, by the ringing of his bell, the attention of the public to the fact that a young philosopher was lost, and to the still more important fact that five shillings would be the reward of his fortunate discoverer. I well remember sitting on the steps of the door of the linendraper's shop on the opposite corner of Tooley Street, when the gold-laced crier was making proclamation of my loss; but I was too much occupied with eating some pears to attend to what he was saying.

The fact was that one of the men in the linendraper's shop, observing a little child by itself, went over to it, and asked what it wanted. Finding that it had lost its nurse, he brought it across the street, gave it some pears, and placed it on the steps at the door: having asked my name, the shopkeeper found it to be that of one of his own customers…

Even as a boy, Babbage loved to know how things worked. What fascinated him from his childhood was the 'desire to enquire into the causes of all those little things and events which astonish the childish mind.' 'My invariable question on receiving any new toy was 'Mamma, what is inside of it?' Until this information was obtained those around me had no repose, and the toy itself… was generally broken open if the answer did not satisfy my own little ideas…'

When the forty-two-year old met seventeen-year-old Ada and Lady Byron for the first time, little had changed. In a passage in his book *On the Economy of Machinery and Manufactures* (1832) Babbage goes into great detail about how the remains of a horse are used economically by selling the hair from the mane to upholsterers, the skin to tanners, the flesh to the animal-meat trade, the fat to soap-makers, the bones to glue-makers and cutlers, and how even the maggots produced in the decomposing flesh are put to use as bait for fishing, though mainly as food for fowls, and (as Babbage notes) 'especially for pheasants'.

The young Babbage's enthusiasm was carefully fanned by his parents. When he was living in London with his parents, his mother took him to several exhibitions of machinery, including one in Hanover Square, organised by a man who called himself 'Merlin'.

I was so greatly interested in it, that the exhibitor remarked the circumstance, and after explaining some of the objects to which the public had access, proposed to my mother to take me up to his workshop, where I should see still more wonderful automata. We accordingly ascended to the attic. There were two uncovered female figures of silver, about twelve inches high.

One of these walked or rather glided along a space of about four feet, when she turned round and went back to her original place. She used an eye-glass occasionally, and bowed frequently, as if recognising her acquaintances. The motions of her limbs were singularly graceful.

The other silver figure was an admirable *danseuse*, with a bird on the forefinger of her right hand, which wagged its tail, flapped its wings, and opened its beak. This lady attitudinised in a most fascinating manner. Her eyes were full of imagination, and irresistible.

These silver figures were the chef d'oeuvres of the artist. They had cost him years of unwearied labour, and were not even then finished, like the engines that Babbage was to design.

Four years after Byron, Babbage attended the same college as Ada's father, Trinity. His Cambridge years couldn't have been further removed from a cauldron of moral turpitude or a pile of mounting debts, however. He keenly played chess and recalls, for example, how he and some friends founded a Ghost Club, designed to collect evidence about the existence of ghosts. They also founded 'a club which they called The Extractors' designed to help its members in the event that any of them were the subject of a petition to get them sent to a lunatic asylum.

His wildest time was a sailing trip of several days during term time:

I was very fond of boating, not of the more manual labour of rowing, but the more intellectual art of sailing. I kept a beautiful light, London built boat, and occasionally took long voyages down the river, beyond Ely into the Fens. To accomplish these trips, it was necessary to have two or three strong fellows to row when the wind failed or was contrary. These were useful friends upon my aquatic expeditions, but not being of exactly the same calibre as my friends of the Ghost Club, were very cruelly and disrespectfully called by them 'my Tom fools'...

I also directed my servant to order the cook to send me a large well-seasoned meat pie, a couple of fowls, etc. These were packed in a hamper with three or four bottles of wine and one of noyeau [Noyaux, almond liqueur]. We sailed when the wind was fair, and rowed when there was none. Whittlesea Mere was a very favourite resort for sailing, fishing and shooting. Sometimes we reached [King's] Lynn.

The truth is that Babbage, having been encouraged in all his enthusiasms, was something of a dilettante. He dabbled, and what was worse, he rather seems to have enjoyed dabbling. Unlike his friend Charles Dickens, his father's money had always cushioned him from the need to ever finish anything. And much like Byron, Babbage had a disdain for making money off his inventions, let alone turning them into a commercial enterprise.

Any goals would be set by Babbage himself. By the time he went up to Trinity College in 1810, Britain was in the midst of its unprecedented technology revolution. Transport, communications and above all the application of steam power to industry were giving mankind the opportunity to use levels of power thousands of times greater than that which the horse, or the human hand, could produce. Babbage felt he would like to take part in that revolution in some capacity or other, so he withdrew from the curriculum for the Senate House Exam and pursued his own mathematical and scientific agenda. At the time, gentlemen scholars were permitted to do this.

With two friends he had met at Cambridge – John Herschel (son of the famous astronomer Sir William Herschel who had in 1871 sensationally discovered Uranus, the first new planet) and one George Peacock – Babbage also helped form what he called the 'Analytical Society'. Its main objective was to overhaul the study of calculus at Cambridge and replace the notation of Newton with what Babbage and his friends regarded as the much more efficient notation invented by Leibniz. The campaign was, in the end, successful, although it would not be won until after Babbage graduated from Cambridge in 1814. (He would later become the eleventh Lucasian Professor in Mathematics at the university; Isaac Newton had been the second holder of this prestigious chair.) But the vigour of the arguments put forward to support the change forced the outside mathematical world to start to take notice of the founders of the Analytical Society, and particularly of Babbage and Herschel. It was an important contribution to science, and one of the few Babbage ever saw through to its end.

The friendship between Babbage and Herschel was the first serious intellectual friendship either had. They were touchingly good companions, and Babbage was to name his oldest son Benjamin, after his father, and Herschel. They addressed each other as 'Dear Herschel' or 'Dear Babbage' in letters: an extremely intimate salutation by the formal standards of the time. The informality of their letters (which usually contained abundant mathematical formulae as well as personal material) is neatly explained by a comment Herschel made at the start of a letter he wrote to Babbage on February 25 1813:

When men with common pursuits in which they are deeply interested, correspond on the subject of those pursuits, the trifling ceremonials of an ordinary correspondence may in great measure be waived.

Babbage's friendship with Herschel frequently sustained and supported Babbage during a life with many setbacks.

While his father was still alive, Babbage pretended to have an interest in earning a living. But he never found any jobs that he either wanted to do, or was appointed to do. Despite moans and complaints, Benjamin gave the couple enough money to live on in reasonable comfort at 5 Devonshire Street, Portland Place, London.

At the same time, Babbage wasted no time in making his mark on the scientific scene. During 1815 – the year of Ada's birth – he gave a series of lectures on astronomy to the Royal Institution. In the spring of 1816 he was elected a member of the Royal Society, a learned assembly of all the great scientists of the land. For the next few years Babbage's work was mainly mathematical. He published more than a dozen mathematical papers, all of which were regarded as highly competent, though not of enormous importance.

Babbage, like Byron, doted on his children but after his wife Georgiana died in 1827 they were farmed out.

Herschel, his eldest son, stayed during the school holidays with Babbage's mother Elizabeth who lived (until 1844) in London. Babbage's beloved only daughter Georgiana (who was two years younger than Ada), also stayed with Babbage's mother at her home at 5 Devonshire Street, a ten minute walk from Babbage's house on Dorset Street.

Although he could easily afford to travel in style, Babbage was not the kind of man to idle time on a frivolous Grand Tour. Instead, Babbage and Herschel had made their first trip to France in 1819, the first of many such excursions they made to exchange information and ideas with French men of science. With Herschel's father Sir William's reputation opening doors for the two young men, they were able to meet several prominent French scientists, mathematicians and astronomers.

It was very likely during this first visit to Paris that Babbage first heard of an ambitious French project undertaken at the turn of the century to make a set of reliable mathematical tables for the French Ordnance Survey.

The project had been overseen by the eminent civil engineer Baron Gaspard de Prony. Despite often being in great jeopardy, he had managed to survive the French Revolution's Reign of Terror mainly due to certain influential revolutionaries – chief among them Lazare Carnot himself, *L'Organisateur de la Victoire'* ('the Organiser of the Victory')– who admired his scientific talents.

The French Ordinance Survey required prodigious amounts of multi-digit multi-plication and it needed accurate tables to simplify and speed up its work. Logarithms (a seventeenth century invention by John Napier) were the short-cut to such otherwise time-consuming multiplications. A logarithm converts each number into a calculation of the number 10. The great advantage of this is that if you look up the logarithms (logs) of the two numbers which you want to multiply, all you need to do is add their two logs together, note this total, and go back to the logarithm tables to see which number has the logarithm you end up with. That number is the product of the multiplication of the two original numbers.

While the principle appears simple, it is easier said than done. The purpose of De Prony's undertaking was to calculate the logarithms of the numbers from 1 to 200,000, a massive undertaking even though 200,000 is not a particularly high number. For any numbers higher than 200,000, French surveyors would be obliged to do the laborious sums manually.

De Prony, not surprisingly, was terrified of failing as the Reign of Terror continued to claim the heads of its victims. It was only when De Prony came across a copy of Adam Smith's *The Wealth of Nations*, published some two decades before in 1776, that he found his answer.

In a famous passage, Adam Smith relates how the productivity of a pin factory he had visited had been maximised by groups of workers specialising in different stages of the production of the pins. One group of workers had, for example, straightened the wire, another cut the wire, another sharpened the tips of the pins, and so on. In this way, Adam Smith explained, the total output of the pin factory would be many times greater than that which could have been produced if each individual worker had handled every stage of the pin-making process.

De Prony decided to use the same principle to make his vast set of tables with the greatest accuracy, and within a reasonable time-frame. After planning his approach carefully, he decided to divide his human calculators into three teams.

The first team would oversee the entire undertaking. This would involve investigating and furnishing the different formulae for each function to be calculated and setting down the simple steps of the calculation process. The team would be made up of half a dozen of the best mathematicians in France, including Carnot himself and Adrien-Marie Legendre (famous for important work on elliptic integrals, which provided basic analytic tools for mathematical physics).

The second team of seven or eight human calculators converted the formulae into key numbers which would be the basis for the actual calculations of the values to be set down in the tables.

The third team consisted of sixty to eighty clerks whose mathematical ability was largely limited to being able to add and subtract. By virtue of the way the huge project was organised, this was all they needed to do in order to perform their necessary calculations. Curiously enough, many of the clerks were former hairdressers to the aristocracy. These hairdressers found themselves unemployed after the Revolution's thirst for decapitation.

The tables produced by De Prony's pioneering technique occupied seventeen large folio volumes and had a reputation for being reliable. Their reliability was such that they were used by the French Army as late as 1940 to assist with calculations relating to surveys of terrain. The tables impressed Babbage enormously.

But even though De Prony's tables were regarded by French mathematicians as an enormously useful asset for more than a century, they were never actually *printed*. Instead, they remained in manuscript form, apparently for cost reasons. Only surveyors at the French Ordinance Survey with access to the original volumes could actually use them.

De Prony's mass-production approach to his enormous calculation assignment struck a chord deep within Babbage's analytical mind. When Babbage developed his first cogwheel calculator, he decided to base his machine on the Method of Differences that would reduce the extremely complex business of tables calculation to its simplest essentials, much as De Prony had. Instead of 6 digits (200,000), he planned his tables to run to up to 30 digits, if ever completed.

Furthermore, Babbage knew about the problems De Prony had experienced with getting his tables printed. Babbage was determined to incorporate a printing mechanism within his machine. This would allow the machine to produce a printed output onto paper automatically, eliminating the possibility of human error. Babbage's plan, in fact, was that the machine itself should make printing plates that could be used as many times as required.

Meeting this challenge, and grappling with the practical and conceptual difficulties it involved, took Babbage into a realm of almost inconceivably complex and original inventiveness, even if it never got further than the seventh part of the machine that Ada first saw in 1833. He started by planning his Difference Engine, he ended by designing what was nothing less than a calculator controlled by punched cards.

12

A Window on the Future

On Monday, December 19 1834, just five days after Ada turned nineteen, she spent a fascinating evening with Babbage, Lady Byron and Mary Somerville. Babbage was thrilled about the extraordinary new horizon that had opened up in his mind, and in his mad-scientist way, he communicated his excitement most successfully to his guests. We can get a good idea of just how excited he was from a journal entry Lady Byron made late that evening.

He spoke about his discovery in metaphorical terms rather than seeking to explain it in precise detail. The first glimpse of his discovery had aroused in his mind a sensation that was something like 'throwing a bridge from the known to the unknown world'. According to Lady Byron's journal, Babbage also said that the breakthrough made him feel that he was standing on a mountain peak and watching mist in a valley below start to disperse, revealing a glimpse of a river whose course he could not follow, but which he knew would be bound to leave the valley somewhere. Writing in her journal, Lady Byron later noted 'I understand it to include means of solving equations that hitherto had been considered unsolvable.'

Babbage's only daughter Georgiana had just died suddenly at the age of seventeen, just over three months earlier on September 26, and he had thrown himself into his work, solving an important mechanical issue of the Difference Machine.[4] Or else he had started on his next machine, the one on which he and Ada were to work together closely, the Analytical Engine.

The genesis of the device Babbage was to call the Analytical Engine – echoing the society he had founded with Herschel at Cambridge – can be traced back to a second paper on the Difference Engine that Babbage had read to the Royal Astronomical Society on December 13 1822, when Ada had just turned seven.

In this paper, he explained to his audience that useful as the Difference Engine was, it was always going to be handicapped by the need to reset the machine for each new set of calculations. The point was that the initial numbers that were entered on the cogwheels, had to be entered into the Difference Engine by hand. Once the Engine was set up, the handle could be turned to ensure that the calculation process went on automatically. In principle, the calculations would follow regularly without further intervention by whoever was operating it. But unfortunately, in some calculations, the results would start to become inaccurate as the table production progressed. The machine wasn't to blame for this. It stemmed from the fact that the calculations were based on a mathematical formula which would not in every case be precisely accurate for every single desired numerical result due to the fact that certain numbers would need to be rounded off as they consisted of an infinite number of decimals (one third is a common division, for example, but as a number the Difference Engine could only approximate it as 0.3333 etc; the number of cogwheels limited the number of 3s and could in any case by definition never be infinite).

What was really needed was a machine that would not feature this continual slight reduction in accuracy; a machine, moreover, that could do far more than simply calculate mathematical tables. He named this new endeavour the Analytical Engine. It would soon supersede the Difference Engine into whose design the government had poured the equivalent of two frigates and Babbage himself more than a decade of his life.

Babbage pursued the notion of the Analytical Engine relentlessly during the months that followed his evening with Ada, Lady Byron and Mary Somerville.

The new machine Babbage envisaged would be enormous, about the size of a small steam locomotive in his day or a large van today. It would have contained perhaps as many as 20,000 cogwheels, some mounted in vertical columns like the Difference Engine but others used in a variety of other configurations. Thousands of gear-shafts, camshafts and power transmission rods would have enabled calculations carried out in one part of the machine to be mechanically relayed to other parts. In sketch-books containing his ideas, he made an enormous number of drawings and diagrams for the Analytical Engine, and completed some small working cogwheel components designed to be used in its mechanism.

Above all, the entire operation of the Analytical Engine would be controlled by a punched-card system. The punched-card system was not Babbage's idea, but – as Babbage freely acknowledged (he was always generous with his credits) – based on the Jacquard loom. It was this part that was to provide an important catalyst for Ada's understanding of what the Analytical Engine could really achieve – an understanding that even eluded Charles Babbage himself.

In the summer of 1834, Ada and Lady Byron had been on a tour of the industrial north of England and had visited many factories that were working at full tilt and saw with their own eyes the immense potential of machinery. They also visited the Midlands and saw printers and ribbon factories in Coventry, where Lady Byron drew a picture of a punched card used to instruct a Jacquard loom.

In the same year, Ada and Lady Byron's friendship with Mary Somerville had begun to blossom in the early spring. It was an exciting friendship for Ada, because by now Mary Somerville was one of the best-known mathematicians in Britain, unlike the well-meaning Dr King whom she prodded for a proper study programme in mathematics. Finally she had found in mathematics the intellectual pursuit that satisfied her.

Babbage also became a fixture during these months; though we can't be certain how often their meetings took place, but there are certainly clues: for example, on Thursday March 19 1834, Ada had written a brief letter to Mary Somerville saying that she hoped to meet Mary on Saturday evening at 'Mr Babbage's'. This appears to be a reference to Babbage's Saturday evening soirees which had started in fact in the 1820s for his family but by the 1830s had become events for guests outside the family. As we shall see, the soirees had their heyday in the 1840s but evidently they were already an important part of Babbage's social life at this stage.

Ada continued to write to Dr William King about mathematical matters at this time. She additionally wrote to Mary with whom her friendship was becoming an increasingly intimate, reminding her on Monday November 8 1834, that she promised to make Mary a cap, and would do so as soon as Ada finished her own bonnet.

Ada even had two pupils of her own: Annabella and Olivia Acheson. Olivia and Annabella were the youngest daughters of one of Lady Byron's friends, Lady Gosford, who went off on health cures with her and had evidently named her youngest daughter after Lady Byron. Ada decided to make the most of her time and teach Annabella and Olivia mathematics. They were, respectively, five and four years older (and were to remain spinsters) than her, but this didn't stop Ada, who wrote confidently:

Remember above all things, that you are not to hurry over anything. There is plenty of time, and if you lay a good & solid foundation, the superstructure will be easy, & delightful to build!

Do not become afraid of my becoming too learned to teach you. The more I know myself, the more pleasure I shall take in going over with you the ground I have myself successfully transversed; I get so eager when I write Mathematics to you, that I forget all about handwriting and everything else. – Your progress is the only thing I desire.
Believe me, Your affectionate & untenable Instructress
Ada Byron

By the end of 1834, the Analytical Engine was not the only thing on Ada's mind. She had turned nineteen on December 10. Lady Byron was determined that the time had come for her daughter to find a husband. It appears that Babbage hovered on the radar. While Ada had rediscovered her passion for mathematics as a result of Babbage, it may well have been that bachelor of seven years Babbage also rediscovered something in himself that he had lost as a widower. It was not uncommon for young women of Ada's age to marry older, wealthy men who had been married before. In many ways Ada was well suited for such a role, from Babbage's perspective. Certainly as their friendship developed after Ada's marriage their letters got increasingly light-hearted and self-confessional, as perhaps it had started more innocently at the beginning. Ada was slowly emerging from her chrysalis and was still physically frail and shy as she was preparing to enter London society. Through his interests Babbage had been able to get around her reserve, despite his gnomic utterances, and, with a fortune of £98,000 and four children who were younger than her, he might perhaps have thought that he had a chance. Immediately after Ada married, Lady Byron thus wrote to her 'but has Babbage cut you since your marriage?'

12 St James Square.

But if Babbage was interested, he was not quite what Lady Byron had in mind. While some of her best friends were middle class, she was decidedly orthodox about blue blood. Others had the better measure. Woronzow Greig writes (well after the fact) 'During the spring of 1835 I suggested to my friend Lord Lovelace, then Lord King, that she would suit him as a wife. He and I had been at college together (Trinity Cambridge, Byron's and Babbage's college) and have continued through life on the most intimate terms.' Whether Greig was involved or not, the spring of 1835, Ada was introduced to William, Lord King, who was thirty years old, on a visit to the Warwickshire home of a Sir John Philips.

William, in a word, was a catch. Even Lady Byron could hardly wish for much more. Lord King hailed from an influential political, social, intellectual and religious background. With a title created in 1725, his was just on the right side of Lady Byron's hundred years watershed. And he came with a number of substantial properties, including Ockham Park, Surrey, the Jacobean family seat (he was Lord King, Baron of Ockham) and Ashley Combe in Somerset. He had also just bought 12 St James Square two years earlier, whose facade he had demolished a year after the marriage to be rebuilt by Cubitt in the style he had seen on his own Grand Tour: opulent, Italianate, with a glamorous staircase and enfilade of rooms that set it quite apart from its severe seventeenth original.

Nor was Ada indifferent to William, who was attractive as well as immensely wealthy. On June 28 1835, less than a fortnight before their marriage, she enthused 'What a happiness it is to feel towards any one what I do towards you, & to feel too that it is reciprocal!'

> … I do not think there can be any earthly pleasure equal to that of reposing perfect trust & confidence in another, more especially when that other is to be one's husband.
>
> I hope, my dear William, that I shall make you a very affectionate and very conscientious wife, & shall fulfil all my duties towards you & towards your family in such a manner as to make you the only return I can make for all I owe you, & of which I am so sure that I shall never be reminded by you, that I must take care to keep the remembrance of it in my head.

While that may still have been written at Annabella's prompting, Ada did take to her marriage with relish. It took place on Wednesday July 8 1835 at Fordhook, after which Ada and William had a honeymoon at their stately home, Ashley Combe in Porlock, near Minehead in Somerset that William had set about renovating in a romantic style. In one letter to William, on Friday evening, October 9 1835, when they were temporarily apart, she describes her pregnancy as 'the commencement of the hatching', and refers to herself as a 'hatch bird.' She adds 'I want my Cock to keep me warm' – William's nickname, chosen by Ada, was 'Cock' – signing off, 'My dearest mate, yours most affectionately.'

In short succession Ada did what was expected, and a son, Byron (the heir), was born on May 12 1836; their daughter, Annabella, on September 22 1837 and she gave birth to a second son, Ralph (the spare), their last child, on July 2 1839. It helped no doubt that loveable, malleable William seems almost from the outset to have accepted that his wife was more intelligent that he was and to have been willing to adopt a fairly subservient position in the relationship. Later in their marriage he would say 'what General you would make!'

But it didn't take Ada too long to realise that William was a somewhat aimless man. He spent a great deal of time and money designing and ordering the construction of tunnels at their country houses. The precise purpose of all these tunnels was never clear. On the accession of Queen Victoria in 1838 he was elevated in the peerage from Baron to Viscount of Ockham, and to the Earldom of Lovelace, an extinct title from Annabella's family the Noels (upon the death of her uncle Lord Wentworth, she and her father had inserted 'Noel' before 'Milbanke'). But rather than rewards for any particular achievements of William's, they appear to have been political pleasantries from the new monarch prompted by one of her ministers. Ada herself would henceforth sign her name 'Ada Lovelace', using her own family name.

Paradoxically, Lady Byron never dropped her husband's name, even when she eventually inherited her uncle's title and became Baroness of Wentworth.

Ashley Combe, Porlock, Somerset.

After a few years of what appears to be genuine happiness, Ada began to find her husband's lack of overall purpose intensely irritating. This was evidently a problem throughout their marriage; one of the letters discovered in the north of England and written by Ada on Christmas Day 1846, amounts to a ticking-off of Babbage for, as she saw it, obstructing the procurement of a possible appointment for William. 'You can have no conception of what my husband is, when his home *alone* occupies his irritable energies,' she writes. She craved a husband who would do great things, be great, stride to fame and illustriousness with her by his side and understand her own pressing needs for an intellectual life. But William was not that man.

Her duty as wife having been dispensed with, Ada resumed her passion for mathematics despite the wealth that surrounded her. She became determined to find a distinguished mathematical and scientific tutor who would guide and accompany her on her intellectual quest. Who better to ask than Babbage?

During the first few years of her marriage, he was often a visitor to Ada and William at their home in Ockham in Surrey. Ada was certainly keen to see him. In one short letter written on March 24, almost certainly in 1839, she chastises him playfully:

Sat[ur]d[a]y next will suit us perfectly, but we hope you will stay on as far into the following week, as possible. Surely the machine allows you a holiday sometimes. –

This charming note sets the tone for how their friendship would develop with Ada often describing herself as 'a fairy'. In November 1839, she writes to Babbage to ask if he could help her find someone to teach her mathematics:

> … quite made up my mind to have some instruction next year in Town, but the difficulty is to find the *man. I* have a peculiar *way* of *learning,* & I think it must be a peculiar man to teach me successfully.-
>
> Do not reckon me conceited, for I am sure I am the very last person to think over-highly of *myself,* but I believe I have the *power* of going just as far as I like in such pursuits, & where there is so very decided a taste, I should almost say a *passion,* as I have for them, I question if there is not always some portion of natural genius even. – At any rate the taste is such that it *must* be gratified. – I mention all this to you because I think you are or may be in the way of meeting with the right sort of person, & I am sure you have at any rate the *will* to give me any assistance in your power.
>
> Lord L [Lovelace] desires all sorts of reminiscences, & that I am to take care & remind you about coming to Ockham. –
> Yours most sincerely,
> Ada Lovelace

When Babbage replied on November 29 1839, he responds, perhaps playfully, to his 'fairy'.

> Dear Lady Lovelace
> I make no most ungrateful returns for your kind letter from London. I have lately been ever more than usually occupied by the Engine.
>
> I allowed myself ten days in Cheshire and finding this did not do I was obliged to go to Brighton for five days which restored me to the calculating state and have been working very hard ever since.
>
> I have just arrived at an improvement which will throw back all my drawings full six months unless I succeed in carrying out some new views which may shorten the labour.
>
> I have now commenced the description of the Engine so that I am fully occupied.
>
> I think your taste for mathematics is so decided that it ought not to be checked. I have been making enquiry but cannot find at present any one at all to recommend to assist you. I will however not forget the search.
>
> The London World is very quiet at present. Mrs De Morgan has just added a new philosopher to its population and Mr Sheridan Knowles has written a most popular play called 'Love' to which I have been a frequent attendant. I

met the author yesterday at a dinner at Mr Rogers'.

I could not by possibility have visited you this year in the West, but I cherish the hope of getting a few days at Ockham when I can indulge in a little recreation.

Pray forgive my epistolary negligence and believe me with best regards to Lord Lovelace.

Ever very sincerely yours.

C Babbage

Knowles's play concerns a countess who is in love with her serf called Huon but her father the duke is opposed to this marriage. Was it intended as an allusion to Babbage's true feelings, and did Ada read it that way?

Ada Lovelace, 1838 (A.E. Chaton, RA).

13

The Jacquard Loom

Ada received Babbage's letter about seeing the play *Love* in December 1839. Whatever she felt exactly about Babbage, in the same month she would write another letter that would have important consequences for their work together.

1839 was not a good year for England. With riots happening almost every day in the countryside and towns over high food prices and low wages, many feared that England was in danger of sliding into anarchy. By modern standards the vast majority of people in Britain were poor; suffering routinely from malnutrition, and illness. The small proportion of the population who were well-fed and privileged slept uneasily in their comfortable beds, only too aware of what happened in France a few decades ago.

So here we are here on a December day at Number One Dorset Street, Babbage's London home. The man himself, forty-seven years old, is sitting at his writing-desk in his study. He takes out his pen, dips it into an inkwell, and starts to write a letter to a Parisian friend.

The particular friend Babbage is writing to is the French astronomer and scientist, François Jean Dominique Arago. Babbage got to know Arago in Paris back in 1819 when he travelled there with John Herschel. Babbage and Arago hit it off at once and had remained friends ever since. When Babbage corresponds with Arago he does so in English, while Arago replies in French. They both understand each other's native languages, but prefer to express themselves in their own.

'My dear sir,' Babbage writes:
I am going to ask you to do me a favour.
    There has arrived lately in London… a work which does the highest credit to the arts of your country. It is a piece of silk in which is woven by means of the Jacard [sic] loom a portrait of M. Jacard sitting in his workshop. It was executed in Lyons as a tribute to the memory of the discoverer of a most admirable contrivance which at once gave an almost boundless extent to the art of weaving.
    It is not probable that that copy will be seen as much as it deserves and my first request is, *if* it can be purchased, that you will do me the favour to procure for me two copies and send them to Mr Henry Bulwer at the English Embassy who will forward them. If, as I fear, this beautiful production is not sold, then I rely on your friendship to procure for me *one* copy by represent-ing in the proper quarter the circumstance which makes me anxious to possess it.

The portrait of Jacquard was indeed fascinating as it was essentially a digitised image. Made using 24,000 punched cards, it wove an image of the inventor of the loom on which it was woven. Babbage had become fascinated by the Jacquard loom and he sensed the importance of the portrait in relation to his own work. Also, back in 1836 he had noted briefly in one of his notebooks that the Jacquard loom punched cards – or rather, cards very much like them – could be utilised to act as a way of – as Babbage expressed it – making the Analytical Engine 'special', by which he meant making it ready to carry out a particular calculation. This terminology of making his machine 'special' was the closest Babbage got to describing the modern concept of programming a computer.

Babbage was so fascinated with the Jacquard loom and the portrait that in the same letter, he asked Arago to send 'any memoir about it which may be published.' Clearly, no information was available to him as yet, as he continued the misspelling of 'M. Jacard'. Money was no object to Babbage, so keen was he to get what he wanted. Although he was misspelling Jacquard's name, he had no misapprehension about the revolution the Jacquard loom had created in the story of technology.

Whatever these things may cost, if you will mention to me the name of your banker in Paris I will gladly pay the amount into his hands and shall still be indebted to you for procuring for me objects of very great interest.

Babbage's letter then proceeds to the hub of the matter. The Englishman explains exactly why he is so fascinated by the Frenchman's work.

You are aware that the system of cards which Jacard [sic] invented are the *means* by which we can communicate to a very ordinary loom orders to weave *any* pattern that may be desired. Availing myself of the same beautiful invention I have by similar means communicated to my Calculating Engine orders to calculate *any* formula however complicated. But I have also advanced one stage further and without making *all* the cards, I have communicated through the same means orders to follow certain *laws* in the use of those cards and thus the Calculating Engine can solve any equations, eliminate between any number of variables and perform the highest operations of analysis.

Among Babbage's many contributions to the birth of information technology, the most significant was that he spotted a way to adapt Jacquard's punched-card programming to a completely new purpose: mathematical calculation.

At a technical level, Babbage really did borrow Jacquard's idea lock, stock and barrel. Babbage saw that just as Jacquard's loom employed punched cards to control the action of small, narrow, circular metal rods which in turn governed the action of individual warp threads, he himself could use the same principle to control the positions of small, narrow, circular metal rods that would govern the settings of cogwheels carrying out various functions in his calculating machine.

Augustus de Morgan.

Ada was at this time still looking for a tutor. In the summer of 1840, Lady Byron came to the rescue. She arranged for her daughter to be instructed by the well-known mathematician and logistician named Augustus de Morgan, another Trinity graduate from Cambridge and friend of Babbage's. Under his guidance, Ada made rapid progress in studying her favourite subject. For the first time in her life she seems to have felt some real intellectual fulfilment. She was relentless in her questions to him. In fact when she fell ill he and his wife Sophia (Frend) wrote with great concern to Lady Byron that Ada's constitution might be temperamentally unsuited to mathematics. The formidable Lady Byron, as well as Lord Lovelace, seem to have promptly disabused De Morgan of that idea in the bud:

> I have received your note and should have answered no further than that I was very glad to find my apprehension… is unfounded in the opinion of yourself and Lord Lovelace who *must* be better than I am.

He didn't want to let it go though and wrote 'at the same time it is very necessary that the one point should be properly stated'. More specifically he was the expert in one thing. He pointed out politely that they knew Ada 'on every point of the case but one, and may be on that one.' Here lay his deep worry: Ada's voracious attack on his subject. She was not satisfied with merely taking lady-like instruction from De Morgan, she questioned him widely, well beyond what he put on her plate and he anxiously avoided encouraging her in this.

I have never expressed to Lady Lovelace my opinion of her as a student of these matters. I always feared that it might promote an application to them which might be injurious to a person whose bodily health is not strong. I have therefore contented myself with very good, quite right, and so on. But I feel bound to tell you that the power of thinking on these matters which Lady L. has always shown from the beginning of my correspondence with her, has been something so utterly out of the common way for any beginner, man or woman, that this power must be duly considered by her friends with reference to the question whether they should urge or check her obvious determination to try not only to reach but to get beyond, the present bound of knowledge.

Putting his point more finely – in a short-hand that both Lady Byron and Lord Lovelace would understand – he rated her performance as if she was a Trinity student. She was unlikely to have gained the top first in her first year at Cambridge (called the senior wrangler).

Had any young beginner, about to go to Cambridge, shown the same power, I should have prophesied first that his aptitude at grasping the strong points and the real difficulties of first principles would have very much lowered his chance of being senior wrangler; secondly, that they would have certainly made him an original mathematical investigator, perhaps of first-rate eminence.

It was the point that followed hereafter that really carried the nub of De Morgan's concern. It reads now as unadultered misogyny, but its sentiment was accepted by most if not all at the time: the concern he really had was that the foundations of science and mathematics should remain out of bounds for women. He wrote this despite the fact that his wife had been extremely well educated by her father, the former Cambridge don William Frend (Ada and Lady Byron's tutor), and was a social reformer – education for women, opposition to vivisection, assistance of 'gutter children' – as well as a journalist and children's writer.

The questions Ada was asking him were simply not appropriate for any woman in the world to ask, not even Mary Somerville – on whose work a recent book of his relied. He might, he writes, allow one exception (but not really): the mathematician Maria Agnesi. She was the author of a huge two-volume work on mathematics in 1748 that had earned her a professorship at the University of Bologna by appointment of Pope Benedict XIV, and she is today credited as the first female mathematician. What really worried De Morgan was the fact that Ada thought like a man:

> All women who have published mathematics hitherto have shown knowledge, and the power of getting it, but no one, except perhaps (I speak doubtfully) Maria Agnesi has wrestled with difficulties and shown a man's strength in getting over them. The reason is obvious: the very great tension of mind which they require is beyond the strength of a woman's physical power of application. Lady L has unquestionably as much power as would require all the strength of a man's constitution to bear the fatigue of thought to which it will unquestionably lead her … . Perhaps you think. that Lady L will, like Mrs Somerville, go on in a course of regulated study, duly mixed with the enjoyment of society, the ordinary cares of life, &c., &c. But Mrs Somerville's mind never led her into other than the details of mathematical work; Lady L will take quite a different route. It makes me smile to think of Mrs Somerville's quiet acquiescence in ignorance of the nature of force… 'and that is all we know about the matter' – and to imagine Lady L reading this, much less writing it. Having now, I think, quite explained that you must consider Lady L's case as a peculiar one I will leave it to your better judgment, supplied with facts, only begging that this note may be confidential.

To their credit, Lady Byron and Lord Lovelace must have been unimpressed. Ada's studies continued.

During the next two years of her life Ada often met Babbage in London, or he came to visit her and William at Ockham. She clearly enjoyed discussing all sorts of puzzles and mathematical problems with Babbage, and in one particular letter she has the first vision of how she might be able to help him with his endeavours with the calculating engines. During this period of her life, she is often very forward towards him and there is a sense of a true intellectual collaboration.

On January 24 1840, Babbage received a reply, in French, to his letter to his friend Arago, who wrote amicably and helpfully:

> My dear friend and colleague
>   I fear that the person from Lyons of whom I have made enquiries for

information about the Jacquard portrait must be out of town. I haven't had any answer to my queries… Please be assured that I will completely fulfil, *con amore*, the commission with which you have charged me. I do not want you to have the slightest reason to doubt the high esteem in which I hold your talents and your character, nor the importance I attach to our friendship.

Your devoted friend Jean Arago.

Arago was as good as his word. He stuck to the task, and by the spring appears to have been successful in obtaining at least one of the woven portraits that Babbage longed to own.

Driven on by curiosity and admiration, Babbage made a personal pilgrimage to Lyons later that year to see Jacquard's loom in action.

The story of Babbage's visit to Lyons contains some intriguing surprises. Buried in the Babbage papers at the British Museum there is an invoice, dated September 8 1840, issued by the French Society for the Manufacture of Fabrics for the Furnishing and Decoration of Churches. This relates to the purchase of a 'tableau' (that is, the woven portrait) of Jacquard produced by the Lyons firm of Didier Petit & Co. The invoice is made out to 'Monsieur Babbage'. It is quite clear that Babbage kept it as a record of having purchased the woven portrait and of how much it cost him. The invoice is for 200 francs. The daily average wage of an artisan in 1840 was about four francs. Comparing wage rates today with 1840, we can conclude that Babbage paid about £4,000 at modern prices for his woven portrait of Jacquard.

It is natural to assume that the invoice in Babbage's papers relates to the woven portrait of Jacquard that Babbage obtained through Arago, and which he put on show at his soirées. But in fact this was *not* the case. Instead, the invoice turns out to be for a *second* portrait of Jacquard that Babbage obtained under rather more exotic circumstances.

In June or July 1840, Babbage had been invited by the Italian mathematician Giovanni Plana to attend a meeting of Italian scientists scheduled to take place in September in Turin, the city Ada and Lady Byron had visited during Ada's continental tour. Babbage was invited to a similar meeting the previous year but had declined, pleading that he was too busy with his work on the Analytical Engine. This time he accepted. Very likely he did so because of the extraordinary insight into the importance of the Analytical Engine shown by Plana in his letter of invitation.

In his autobiography, Babbage recalls:

In 1840 I received from my friend M Plana a letter pressing me strongly to visit Turin at the then approaching meeting of Italian philosophers. M. Plana stated that he had enquired anxiously of many of my countrymen about the power and mechanism of the Analytical Engine. He remarked that from all the information he could collect the case seemed to stand thus:

'Hitherto the *legislative* department of our analysis has been all-powerful – the *executive* all feeble. Your engine seems to give us the same control over the executive which we have hitherto only possessed over the legislative department.'

Considering the exceedingly limited information which could have reached my friend respecting the Analytical Engine, I was equally surprised and delighted at this exact prevision of its powers.

Plana's comment in effect amounted to a recognition that the Analytical Engine might be able to solve the long-standing problem of the lack of processing power to evaluate complex mathematical formulae. It was an extraordinarily far-sighted observation, and it is hardly surprising that Babbage was so thrilled at Plana's perceptiveness.

The German Romantic poet and philosopher Novalis once remarked: 'It is certain my conviction gains infinitely, the moment another soul will believe in it.' This could be a motto for all of Babbage's life; it explains much of his behaviour, especially during the long and often lonely years when he was working on his cogwheel computers. With no efficient working version of a Difference Engine or Analytical Engine to show the world, he was obliged to seek what seemed the next-best thing; the society of those who seemed to understand what he was trying to do. The fact that he was prepared to travel all the way to Italy – a far from easy journey in 1840, even for a man of Babbage's financial resources and energy, suggests how cut off from empathy and support at home he perceived himself to be.

Very possibly he was also influenced in his decision to make the journey by the fact that the journey to Turin offered Babbage an ideal opportunity to visit Lyons on the way, and find out more about Joseph-Marie Jacquard. The Lyons silk industry had sprung up there partly because of the city's proximity to Italy, and now Babbage was exploiting that very fact to combine his excursion to Turin with a visit to Lyons.

As things transpired, the trip to Turin led directly to a development that put Ada at the centre-stage of the computer revolution that very nearly took place in Britain in the midst of the nineteenth century.

Babbage left England for Paris in the middle of August 1840. In the capital, he collected letters of introduction from Arago and other friends to people in Lyons.

A few days later he arrived in Jacquard's birthplace. As he relates in *Passages*:

On my road to Turin I had passed a few days at Lyons, in order to examine the silk manufacture. I was especially anxious to see the loom in which that admirable specimen of fine art, the portrait of Jacquard, was woven. I passed many hours in watching its progress.

If you wanted to be part of the scientific and literary set in the London of the 1840s, you would have done just about anything to beg, steal or borrow an invitation to one of Babbage's soirées.

Charles Dickens, 1838 (Samuel Laurence).

Babbage had moved to Dorset Street in 1828 after the death of his wife. For the first few years his parties there were private functions for family and close friends. But in the early 1830s, as he needed influential allies, he broadened the list of guests to include many of the leading luminaries of British intellectual life.

During the next decade his social events became renowned throughout the capital. They frequently lasted until well after midnight, under the glow of thousands of candles. Three hundred guests, or even more, might attend. Invitations were so prized that even some of the most famous people in London used to write begging letters to Babbage to try to secure an invitation for themselves, their family or friends.

By this time the soirées were becoming one of the great rendezvous points for liberal intellectuals in Victorian London. Charles Dickens, Charles Darwin, the actor William Macready, the scientist Henry Fitton and his wife, the geologist Charles Lyell, the self-taught mathematician Mary Somerville and her family, the anatomist Richard Owen, the magistrate William Broderip, the astronomer Sir John Herschel, and of course Ada; these are just a few of the 'names' who were often to be found at

Babbage's parties. George Ticknor, a man of letters from the United States, describes a visit to one of Babbage's parties on May 26 1838.

> About eleven o'clock we got away from Lord Fitzwilliam's and went to Mr Babbage's. It was very crowded tonight, and very brilliant; for among the people there were Hallam, Milman and his pretty wife; the Bishop of Norwich, Stanley, the Bishop of Hereford, Musgrave, both the Hellenists; Rogers, Sir J. Herschel and his beautiful wife, Sedgwick, Mrs Somerville and her daughters, Senior, the Taylors, Sir F. Chantrey, Jane Porter, Lady Morgan [the novelist], and I know not how many others. We seemed really to know as many people as we should in a party at home, which is a rare thing in a strange capital, and rarest of all in this vast overgrown London. Notwithstanding, therefore, our fatiguing day, we enjoyed it very much.

The Difference Engine was eight years long the most prominent conversation piece at his glittering events. But he also delighted in entertaining the guests who came to his soirées with ingenious devices and gimmicks.

Thus, in the spring of 1840, Babbage started exhibiting something else: the almost miraculous woven portrait of Jacquard. The woven portrait shows the inventor sitting in a luxurious cushioned chair at his work bench. He is holding a pair of callipers against long strips of cardboard that have tiny holes punched in them. The bench also accommodates a model of a loom. Hanging up on a rack on a wall behind the inventor are chisels and other tools in a variety of shapes and sizes. Rolled-up plans are poking out of a drawer on a table beneath the rack.

The portrait gives the impression of being an informal snapshot of the inventor as he momentarily turns away from his work and glances at the artist. He has a thoughtful, frowning air about him, and his well-cut coat and general air of prosperity suggest that this is an inventor who has enjoyed some success.

Babbage enjoyed showing the portrait to his guests. He would then ask them how they thought it had been made. When they told him they thought it was an engraving, as they usually did, he gave a knowing smile.

One evening in 1842, two of the most distinguished people in the realm had attended a Babbage soirée. They were the Duke of Wellington and Prince Albert, Queen Victoria's husband. The 'Iron Duke' was, of course, the hero of Waterloo and a former Prime Minister. Prince Albert was famous for his intellect and the important, even essential, role he played in governing Britain. Officially he had no power, but in practice the Queen deferred to his judgement and opinion on almost every matter. She usually succeeded in persuading her ministers to do the same.

Almost as soon as the Duke and the Prince arrived, Babbage showed them the portrait. The Prince asked Babbage why he thought the portrait so important. Babbage replied, in characteristically enigmatic fashion, 'it will greatly assist in explaining the nature of my calculating machine the Analytical Engine.'

Once the two guests had examined the portrait, Babbage asked them what they thought it was. The Duke of Wellington made the usual mistake of responding that it must be an engraving. But it turned out the Prince knew the truth, having apparently heard of the portrait before. He informed the Duke of Wellington that the portrait was not an engraving at all, but a woven piece of fabric.

A few originals of the woven portrait still exist today. As we gaze into Jacquard's stern features, it is difficult to believe that this faded, rather small picture (it only measures 20 inches by 14), could have had such a prodigious effect on Ada's imagination, but it did. It's no exaggeration to say that without this woven portrait, Ada would almost certainly have never had the insight she did not only into Babbage's Analytical Engine, but into her dream of what a computer could be.

Babbage returned to Britain in September 1840. Temporarily exhilarated by his visit to Turin, where he had been received as an eminent international scientist and inventor, he had to confront the depressing truth that it was increasingly unlikely he would ever be able to afford to build the Analytical Engine. He knew that his own financial resources, considerable as they were, would be nowhere near enough for the task. Yet somehow he continued to apply himself with energy and dedication to his great object.

Luigi Federico Menabrea.

He was sustained by two hopes.

Firstly, he thought it reasonably likely that one of the Italian scientists whom he had recently visited might write a lengthy and detailed paper on the new project.

Babbage hoped that such a paper would affirm the importance of the invention and give him leverage with the British Government who had so generously supported him with the construction of the Difference Engine. He had a curious habit of trying to win influence by these rather indirect means instead of honing his diplomatic skills and adopting a more direct, and possibly more successful, approach.

His host in Turin, Giovanni Plana, had indicated that he himself was not in sufficiently good health enough to undertake the job, but Luigi Federico Menabrea, a talented young mathematician whom Plana had introduced to Babbage in Turin, appeared interested in carrying it out. Babbage remained in touch with Menabrea and supplied him with comprehensive information about the Analytical Engine. It was this connection with Menabrea that was soon to lead to the involvement of Ada Lovelace.

Babbage's second cause for optimism, however tenuous, was that the Government might, after all, have a spontaneous change of heart and make new funding available to him. This was something he intended to advance. It may well be that in his mind the idea had formed that Ada's involvement could in some way help his indirect campaign to spread the word about his new Engine.

Meanwhile, he had his friendship with Ada to enjoy. Here, for example, is a letter she wrote to Babbage on Tuesday January 12 1841. She was very keen to be involved with his plans, and pressed him on this whenever she could.

My Dear Babbage.
If you will come by the *Railway* on Friday, we will send the carriage to meet you at *Weybridge*, for the Train that leaves Town about 4 o'clock & arrives at Weybridge a few minutes before 5 o'clock.

Bring warm coats or cloaks, as the carriage will be probably an open one.

If you are a *Skater*, pray bring *Skates* to Ockham; that being the fashionable occupation here now, & one *I* have much taken to.

I am very anxious to talk to you. I will give you a hint on *what*. It strikes me that at some future time, (it might be even within 3 or 4 years, or it might be *many* years hence), *my head* may be made by you subservient to some of *your* purposes & plans. If so, *if* ever I could be worthy or capable of being *used* by you, my head will be yours. And it is on this that I wish to speak most seriously to you. You have always been a kind and real & most invaluable friend to *me*; & I would that I could in any way repay it, though I scarcely dare so exalt myself as to hope however humbly, that I can ever be intellectually worthy to attempt serving *you*.
Yours most sincerely
A.A. Lovelace
You *must* stay some days with us. Now don't contradict me.

Six weeks later Ada returned to her fashionable, modern, Cubitt-designed house on St James whose renovation had evidently already been completed. She urged Babbage to visit at once and mentioned with mounting excitement that they will embark on a project together.

Monday, 22 February,

Ockham Park

My Dear Mr Babbage

We are to move to Town on Thursday; & I hope to see you as soon afterwards as you like, – the sooner the better.

Remember that *one* o'clock is the best hour for a call. –

I believe I shall perhaps pass Sunday Evening with Mr & Mrs De Morgan [Augustus and Sophia (Frend)]; but this is not yet quite fixed, & if it should not take place, will *you* come & spend it in St James' Sqre – You see I am determined to celebrate the Sabbath *Mathematically*, in one way or other. -

I have been at work very strenuously since I saw you, & quite as successfully as heretofore. I am now studying attentively the *Finite Differences*… And in this I have more particular interest, because I know it bears directly on some of *your* business. – Altogether I am going on well, & just as we might have anticipated. -

I think I am more determined than ever in my future plans; and I have quite made up my mind that nothing must be suffered to interfere with them. – I intend to make such arrangements in Town as will secure me a couple of hours daily (with very few exceptions), for my studies.

I think much of the possible (I believe I may say the *probable*) future connection between *us*; and it is an anticipation I increasingly like to dwell on. I think great good may be the result to *both* of us; and I suspect that the idea, (which by the bye is one that I believe I have *long* entertained, in a vague and crude form), was one of those happy instincts which do occur to one sometimes so unaccountably & fortunately. At least, in my opinion, the results *may* ultimately prove it such.

Believe me

Yours most sincerely

Ada Lovelace

A Mind with a View

Luigi Federico Menabrea's paper on the Analytical Engine might have stayed as
obscure as the learned Swiss journal in which it was published had not Ada decided
that translating it into English would neatly achieve two objects that she considered
close to her heart.

Firstly, it would give her the opportunity to publicise the important work being
done by her close friend Babbage, of whom she was seeing a good deal more than
ever before.

Secondly, the translation work would allow her to advance her dream of having
an intellectual career which would lift her above the demands of motherhood,
running three homes and looking after a wealthy but ineffectual husband.

Ada was conscious of the difficulty of her task, but was convinced that she was
more than equal to the job. She launched into it with characteristic energy. Her French
was excellent, and her best writing has a fluency, clarity of expression and mastery of
metaphor and image that on occasion even recalls her father's fluent and expressive
prose. There is no reason to disbelieve Babbage's account in his autobiography that it
was Ada's idea to produce the translation in the first place. Here is what Babbage says
in *Passages from the Life of a Philosopher*. Babbage calls Menabrea's article a 'memoir',
presumably after *Scientific Memoirs* in which Ada's translation was published in 1843:

> Some time after the appearance of his memoir on the subject in the *Bibliothèque
> Universelle de Genève*, the late Countess of Lovelace informed me that she had
> translated the memoir of Menabrea. I asked why she had not herself written
> an original paper on a subject with which she was so intimately acquainted? To
> this Lady Lovelace replied that the thought had not occurred to her. I then
> suggested that she should add some notes to Menabrea's memoir: an idea
> which was immediately adopted.

In many ways this passage is telling. It was written by a man who was convinced
of his own abilities. From his early youth he had been coddled, encouraged, and told
he was brilliant – which he undoubtedly was. Only months earlier to the events he
describes he had, as we shall see, almost verbally assaulted a man he'd never met and
whose views he didn't know but whose support he nonetheless sought. Ada was
undoubtedly gifted, but had been told from early youth to not think too much of
herself – as was common for rich aristocratic girls surrounded by tutors and
governesses – lest it encourage the wilful parts of her personality. She was highly
intelligent and used to getting her way as she grew older and less timid. In science, her

confidence melted away and she saw her role as that of the hand-maiden to others. Even her close friendship with the highly respected scientist Mary Somerville had made little difference on what Ada thought of herself. Babbage was surprised by her suggestion to translate Menabrea's essay, and seems to have thought she knew enough about his invention to be able to write an article of her own. The confidence Babbage expressed in her abilities appears not to have convinced Ada, however. She decided to go ahead with a translation, aided by Babbage.

> We discussed together the various illustrations that might be introduced: I suggested several, but the selection was entirely her own. So also was the algebraic working out of the different problems, except, indeed, that relating to the numbers of Bernoulli, which I had offered to do to save Lady Lovelace the trouble. This she sent back to me for an amendment, having detected a grave mistake which I had made in the process.

Instead of writing her own article, what she did was append Menabrea's article with notes that exceeded the length of the translation several times over.

> The notes of the Countess of Lovelace extend to about three times the length of the original memoir. Their author has entered fully into almost all the very difficult and abstract questions connected with the subject.

It has been suggested by some modern – mostly male – writers that the translation and notes were really the work of Babbage's. Certainly he stood to gain from an extended article as the two parts together showed the entire operation of the machine.

> The two memoirs taken together furnish, to those who are capable of understanding the reasoning, a complete demonstration – *That the whole of developments and operations of analysis are now capable of being executed by machinery.*[Babbage's italics.]

It is, however, hard to see why one would want to rob Ada Lovelace of the authorship of her article and Babbage of the sincerity of his memoirs. It seems out of character for a man such as Babbage to inflate his Analytical Engine in a backhanded way. If he had truly wished to see the article translated no doubt he would have been able to find an established scientist through his popular soirées. Moreover, if he had concocted this elaborate lie why exclude the 'working out of... the numbers of Bernoulli.' This is quite apart from the ample linguistic and epistolary evidence suggesting that her writings on the machine were her own. There seems little doubt that he was closely involved and no doubt read her work as it progressed, but peer-review is common in scientific writing. Few would want to claim that PhD theses do not contain the ideas of the candidates themselves.

Babbage's own attempts to advance the interests of the Analytical Engine had encountered a major disaster. A particularly unfortunate example of this was his meeting, on Friday November 11 1842, with the Prime Minister, Sir Robert Peel. Babbage was trying to obtain government funds to complete the machine. The meeting took place not long after Prince Albert's visit and perhaps his intercession had helped Babbage to secure a meeting with the most powerful man in Britain at that moment.

The interview was an unmitigated catastrophe for Babbage. It is possible to reconstruct it almost on a minute-by-minute basis from a detailed account Babbage wrote of the interview. The word 'wrote' is in fact not really adequate to describe how it came to be composed. Immediately after the interview, in a hot fury of anger and disappointment, Babbage rushed back into his house, dashed into his study and – as if aware this was the only way he could obtain any relief – gouged onto paper a blow-by-blow account of what he must even at the time have realised was a meeting that pretty well killed his twenty-year vision of cogwheel computing stone dead.

The document containing the account is lodged in the British Library in London. It is both deeply moving and profoundly troubling.

What Babbage wrote is how what might have been never was. Had the meeting been successful, the seeds would have been sown for the start of an information technology revolution in Victorian Britain. The ways in which technology might have accelerated, and history run differently, over the course of almost two centuries are too enormous to contemplate.

Babbage's vivid account of the meeting includes much of the verbatim dialogue between the two men. His pain and upset are even apparent in the appearance of the writing itself, which is hastily scrawled out and not easy to decipher, and in its syntax. Uncharacteristically for him, in his haste and anger his description of the meeting leaves out much of the punctuation and even some of the words. But he does provide a verbatim account of some of the conversation, so here we have some attest dialogue that can be set down.

The timing of the meeting was, from any perspective, extremely unfortunate. The year 1842 had been a truly tough one for Peel. Shortly before the day when he met Babbage, Peel had written to his wife Julia that he was 'fagged to death,' with the cares of office. Much of the population – whether working in towns or on the land – was permanently close to starvation. Hunger and rioting were widespread.

Peel was in no mood to meet Babbage at all, let alone in the mood for a stressful confrontation with a mad scientist. Babbage would have done much better if he had handled the meeting in a radically different manner. He should have been to the point, pleasant, placatory, and done his utmost to explain his work to Peel in language that presented the practical function to Britain's economy of his invention. As it was, and this is clear even from Babbage's own notes, he conducted the meeting in a defensive, sullen, bad-tempered, querulous, self-centred and self-pitying manner that would only irritate and alienate Peel. As Babbage explains in his account of the interview he began somewhat irrelevantly telling Peel how his detractors might see him:

> I informed Sir RP that many circumstances had at last forced upon me the conviction, which I had long resisted, that there existed amongst men of science great jealousy of me. I said that I had been reluctantly forced to this conclusion of which I now had ample evidence, which however I should not state unless he asked me. In reply to some observation of Sir RP in a subsequent part of the conversation I mentioned one circumstance that within a few days the Secretary of one of the foreign embassies in London has incidentally remarked to me that he had long observed a great jealousy of me in certain classes of English Society.

Babbage went on to explain why he was mentioning all this. He told Peel of his fears that some of those who had advised the Government over the worth of the Engines might have based their decision on personal malice rather than on an objective assessment. Peel evidently made no direct reply to this.

Then, finally, Babbage got down to what really mattered:

> I turned to the next subject, the importance of the Analytical Engine. I stated my own opinion that in the future scientific history of the present day it would probably form a marked epoch and that much depended upon the result of this interview. I added that the Difference Engine was only capable [of] applications to one limited part of science (although that part was certainly of great importance and capable of more immediate practical applications than any other) but the Analytical Engine embraced the whole science.
>
> I stated that it was in fact already invented and that it exceeded any anticipations I had ever entertained respecting the powers of applying machinery to science.

The brilliance of Babbage's anticipation how posterity would see the Analytical Engine uncannily reflects the view of him currently, a time when even the smallest computer has a digital version of what he proposed.

Yet as far as his dealings with the pragmatist Peel were concerned, the problem was that Peel had no real idea what the difference was between the Difference Engine and the Analytical Engine. Peel had no doubt been clearly briefed that the Difference Engine had swallowed up funding equal to two frigates and that it was a technological boat whose inventor himself had decided would never sail. Babbage would surely have done better to have given Peel a clear indication of the practical benefits of his machines, accompanied by a realistic plan of action and a date when the Government could expect that something of definite practical usefulness would be completed, and how completing the Difference Engine would cost more than completing the Analytical Engine – or something to that effect.

But Babbage, in his bitterness and haste to justify himself, tried quoting to Peel the comment Plana had made that the invention of the Analytical Engine would provide 'the same control over the executive [department of analysis] as we have hitherto had over the legislative'. Again, it is difficult to imagine that Peel had the faintest idea what Babbage was talking about. And even if Peel had been carefully briefed, why the British taxpayer should invest a substantial amount of money in furtherance of an obscure statement by an obscure Italian mathematician.

After another bad-tempered, irrelevant and unpleasant discussion, initiated by Babbage, about the different pensions and grants given to scientists by the Government, Peel finally decided to interrupt the endless stream of complaints and grievances and call Babbage to order with a hard fact:

'Mr Babbage, by your own admission you have rendered the Difference Engine useless by inventing a better machine.' Babbage took the bait and glared at Peel. 'But if I finish the Difference Engine it will do even more than I promised. It is true that it has been superseded by better machinery, but it is very far from being 'useless.' The general fact of machinery being superseded in several of our great branches of manufacture after a few years is perfectly well known.'

Only briefly diverted from his spilling his spleen, Babbage again went on to complain of all the vexation and loss of reputation he considered that he had suffered from those members of the public who believed him to have profited personally from the money the Government had granted towards the development of the Difference Engine. 'This belief is so prevalent that several of my intimate friends have asked if it were not true,' Babbage said. 'I have even met with it at the hustings at Finsbury.'

Peel was on home territory now. 'You are too sensitive to such attacks, Mr Babbage,' he replied. 'Men of sense never care for them.'

Fixing the Prime Minister with another hard stare, Babbage finally showed the wit that his friends loved and might have got Peel on side if by now a river of bile didn't flow between them:

Sir Robert, in your own experience of public life you must have frequently observed that the best heads and highest minds are often the most susceptible of annoyance from the injustice or the ingratitude of the public.

Peel was exhausted, and irritated with Babbage. Babbage felt hurt, betrayed, and angry that the Prime Minister could be so reluctant to support the continued development of machines whose worth seemed to Babbage at any rate self-evident.

One wonders to an extent whether Babbage's bluster might have been partly due to the fact that, unlike the Difference Machine which was directly inspired by De Prony's work for the French Ordinance Survey, he found it less easy in his own mind to see the exact point of the far more open-ended Analytical Engine beyond its pure mathematical use.

'I consider myself to have been treated with great injustice by the Government,' was Babbage's unhelpful parting comment, 'But as you are of a different opinion, I cannot help myself.'

Babbage got up from his chair, wished his Prime Minister good morning, and abruptly left the room.

Presumably Ada very quickly heard from Babbage about Peel's rejection. We can readily imagine Ada being sympathetic, but what happened when Babbage met Peel can only have reinforced Ada's conviction that Babbage needed some significant help to advance the interests of the Analytical Engine in the circles of influential people Babbage needed on his side. We can see this clearly from the period from June to September 1843, which is the best documented one of Ada's friendship with Babbage.

After Menabrea's article was published in the Swiss journal *Bibliothèque Universelle de Genève* in October 1842, Babbage is known to have scribbled a personal note in his own papers on February 7 1843, stating that he had had a meeting with Ada 'under new circumstances'. While it seems likely that this was relating to Ada's involvement in the Menabrea translation, we can't know this for certain. It could also be his dashed hopes after the disastrous meeting with Peel. Ada did not start work on her own, additional, material until May or June, but it seems likely that by February 1843 she had drafted her translation of Menabrea's article.

Ada's translation sets out clearly the background of Babbage's new Engine and explains how even the finest mathematical minds have been unable to translate even simple mathematics into a machine that executes in numbers what mathematicians describe on paper in mathematical symbols.

The rigid exactness of those laws which regulate numerical calculations must frequently have suggested the employment of material instruments, either for executing the whole of such calculations or for abridging them; and thence have arisen several inventions having this object in view.

For instance, the much-admired machine of Pascal is now simply an object of curiosity, which, whilst it displays the powerful intellect of its inventor, is yet of little utility in itself. Its powers extended no further than the execution of the first four operations of arithmetic, and indeed were in reality confined to that of the first two, since multiplication and division were the result of a series of additions and subtractions.

The chief drawback hitherto on most of such machines is, that they require the continual intervention of a human agent to regulate their movements, and thence arises a source of errors; so that, if their use has not become general for large numerical calculations, it is because they have not in fact resolved the double problem which the question presents, that of *correctness* in the results, united with *economy* of time.

The text continues to underline the significance of and credits Babbage with 'the realisation of a gigantic idea.' His machine was 'capable of executing not merely arithmetical calculations, but even all those of analysis.'

What is meant here is the field of mathematics that is called analytical (or Leibnizian) calculus, which the Analytical Society that Babbage had been part of had so successfully introduced at Cambridge University. This type of mathematics works with numbers that are infinite (beyond expression in digits) or numbers whose fraction is infinitely small and can never be expressed in sufficient number of digits. A mere calculating machine, such as the original Difference Engine, would only be able to start with incomplete numbers and its calculations would therefore by definition be next to useless to cover this important area of mathematics.

If Babbage could have got it to work on cogwheels, the Analytical Engine would have been amazing. This new machine would in effect be able to work correctly both with exact numbers as well as 'imaginary' numbers, that is to say numbers you can only approximate and never express exactly in reality.

The imagination is at first astounded at the idea of such an undertaking; but the more calm reflection we bestow on it, the less impossible does success appear, and it is felt that it may depend on the discovery of some principle so general, that, if applied to machinery, the latter may be capable of mechanically translating the operations which may be indicated to it by algebraical notation.

Ada did not need to be a genius mathematician to translate Menabrea's article itself, but she did need to have a good understanding of what Menabrea was talking about, and also – this is not a trivial observation – she obviously needed to love the subject of the Analytical Engine, or she would hardly have wanted to do the translation in the first place.

Altogether, Menabrea's translation is about 8,000 words in length. It may seem short, but given the number of mathematical formulas and highly technical detail it is a dense and rich brew, so much so that the article contains one small error in the translation that neither Ada nor Babbage picked up. The French original reads at some point '*Cependant, lorsque le cos de* …' It should have read '*Cependant, lorsque le cas de* …*' But the printer had swapped the French word 'cas' with the word 'cos', a mathematical symbol. The result is something that leads to mathematical gibberish in the context of the machine, which some have used to argue against Ada's brilliance, though not in the same breath against Babbage's – perhaps because it would be hard to defend the claim in the face of his well-documented achievements in so many areas other than the Analytical Engine, his lifetime project.

Babbage's reference to Ada in *Passages* was supplemented, and indeed complemented, by a paragraph he wrote to Ada's son Byron on June 14 1857, nearly five years after Ada's death, and seven years before *Passages* was published. In the letter Babbage observed to Byron Lovelace:

> In the memoir of Mr Menabrea and still more in the excellent Notes appended by your mother you will find the only comprehensive view of the powers of the Analytical Engine which the mathematicians of the world have yet expressed.

Ada appended her own writing about the Analytical Engine as *Notes by the Translator* immediately following her translation of Menabrea's article. Ada's own material has come to be known as her *Notes*. There are seven of them, given successive letters from A to G. Altogether the *Notes* are about 20,000 words long, more than twice as long as the translation.

It is important to point out that much of the content of Ada's *Notes* is highly technical material about how the Analytical Engine is designed to operate and carry out its functions.

However, in addition to technical writings, Ada's *Notes* include general observations about the Analytical Engine. It is these that show the real nature of Ada's achievement in an accessible way.

This passage, close to the beginning of Ada's *Notes*, shows her her passion for explaining in succinct terms to the world what Babbage's Analytical Engine is, and what it means:

> In studying the action of the Analytical Engine, we find that the peculiar and independent nature of the considerations which in all mathematical analysis belong to *operations*, as distinguished from *the objects operated upon* and from the *results* of the operations performed upon those objects, is very strikingly defined and separated.
>
> It is well to draw attention to this point, not only because its full appreciation is essential to the attainment of any very just and adequate general comprehension of the powers and mode of action of the Analytical Engine, but also because it is one which is perhaps too little kept in view in the study of mathematical science in general.
>
> It is, however, impossible to confound it with other considerations, either when we trace the manner in which that engine attains its results, or when we

prepare the data for its attainment of those results.

It were much to be desired, that when mathematical processes pass through the human brain instead of through the medium of inanimate mechanism, it were equally a necessity of things that the reasonings connected with *operations* should hold the same just place as a clear and well-defined branch of the subject of analysis, a fundamental but yet independent ingredient in the science, which they must do in studying the engine.

The confusion, the difficulties, the contradictions which, in consequence of a want of accurate distinctions in this particular, have up to even a recent period encumbered mathematics in all those branches involving the consideration of negative and impossible quantities, will at once occur to the reader who is at all versed in this science, and would alone suffice to justify dwelling somewhat on the point, in connection with any subject so peculiarly fitted to give forcible illustration of it as the Analytical Engine.

What Ada is emphasising here is the clear distinction between data and processing: a distinction we tend to take for granted today, but which – like so much of her thinking about computers – was in her own day not only revolutionary but truly visionary. In none of Babbage's writings does he consider that the new Engine might be used for anything other than mathematics. He himself, with slight condescension, acknowledges this by calling Ada his 'interpretess.'

Ada continues:

It may be desirable to explain, that by the word *operation*, we mean *any process which alters the mutual relation of two or more things*, be this relation of what kind it may. This is the most general definition, and would include all subjects in the universe.

In abstract mathematics, of course operations alter those particular relations which are involved in the considerations of number and space, and the *results* of operations are those peculiar results which correspond to the nature of the subjects of operation.

But the science of operations, as derived from mathematics more especially, is a science of itself, and has its own abstract truth and value; just as logic has its own peculiar truth and value, independently of the subjects to which we may apply its reasonings and processes.

Ada is here seeking to do nothing less than invent the science of computing, and separate it from the science of mathematics. What she calls 'the science of operations' is indeed in effect computing.

Unlike Babbage, Ada saw the practical uses of the Analytical Engine and foresaw the digitisation of music as CDs or synthesisers and their ability to generate music.

The operating mechanism can even be thrown into action independently of any object to operate upon (although of course no *result* could then be developed).

Again, it might act upon other things besides *number*, were objects found whose mutual fundamental relations could be expressed by those of the abstract science of operations, and which should be also susceptible of adaptations to the action of the operating notation and mechanism of the engine.

Supposing, for instance, that the fundamental relations of pitched sounds in the science of harmony and of musical composition were susceptible of such expression and adaptations, the engine might compose elaborate and scientific pieces of music of any degree of complexity or extent.

This most impressive passage shows how Ada sees mathematics and its relationship to philosophy in general. The Cambridge academic and novelist C.P. Snow in 1959 would lament in a lecture called The Two Cultures that our society divides itself into science or the humanities. But in this passage the daughter of Byron – perhaps to the horror of modern poets – writes that mathematics provides the invisible threads that can express everything in the tangible world. Here she leaps well beyond Babbage's Analytical Engine and how it expressed mathematics in the real world, to a philosophical topic that is hotly debated by leading scientists today, and advanced practically by the increasing sophistication of software companies such as Google, who are mining an ever-expanding ocean of data that no human could ever generate.

Those who view mathematical science, not merely as a vast body of abstract and immutable truths, whose intrinsic beauty, symmetry and logical completeness, when regarded in their connection together as a whole, entitle them to a prominent place in the interest of all profound and logical minds, but as possessing a yet deeper interest for the human race, when it is remembered that this science constitutes the language through which alone we can adequately express the great facts of the natural world, and those unceasing changes of mutual relationship which, visibly or invisibly, consciously or unconsciously to our immediate physical perceptions, are interminably going on in the agencies of the creation we live amidst: those who thus think on mathematical truth as the instrument through which the weak mind of man can most effectually read his Creator's works, will regard with especial interest all that can tend to facilitate the translation of its principles into explicit practical forms.

This 158-word sentence is very likely one of the longest sentences in the history of science, but it is also one of the most intriguing. Ada succeeds in this one sentence in linking mathematics, science, religion and philosophy.

In the next passage, which follows immediately on from the above, Ada's grasp of the vital point that the Analytical Engine and the Jacquard loom are, at heart, doing the same kind of thing is a wonderful and enormous conceptual leap that stakes her claim to be a major figure – and unquestionably the leading female figure – in the prehistory of the computer. It shows that she understood exactly what a computer was.

In a terse paragraph she explains (perhaps better than Babbage ever could, who as designer saw many trees but perhaps no longer the forest itself) the essential relationship between the Analytical Engine and the Jacquard loom and how it is different from the earlier invention.

> The distinctive characteristic of the Analytical Engine… is the introduction into it of the principle which Jacquard devised for regulating, by means of punched cards, the most complicated patterns in the fabrication of brocaded stuffs…
>
> The bounds of *arithmetic* were however outstepped the moment the idea of applying the cards had occurred; and the Analytical Engine does not occupy common ground with mere 'calculating machines.'
>
> It holds a position wholly its own; and the considerations it suggests are most interesting in their nature. In enabling mechanism to combine together *general* symbols in successions of unlimited variety and extent, a uniting link is established between the operations of matter and the abstract mental processes of the *most abstract* branch of mathematical science.

In perhaps one of the most visionary sentences written during the entire nineteenth century, she lays out what these cards shall be capable of doing by way of programming the machine. Like the pins of Adam Smith, it is hard to imagine how a simple piece of brocade ever went further in history.

> A new, a vast, and a powerful language is developed for the future use of analysis, in which to wield its truths so that these may become of more speedy and accurate practical application for the purposes of mankind than the means hitherto in our possession have rendered possible. Thus not only the mental and the material, but the theoretical and the practical in the mathematical world, are brought into more intimate and effective connection with each other.
>
> We are not aware of its being on record that anything partaking in the nature of what is so well designated the *Analytical* Engine has been hitherto proposed, or even thought of, as a practical possibility, any more than the idea

of a thinking or of a reasoning machine.

She also addresses succinctly the question that had exercised Prime Minister Robert Peel, who may have wondered what all the fuss was about as both Engines generated numbers (or what Ada calls 'numerical notation').

> Many persons who are not conversant with mathematical studies, imagine that because the business of the engine is to give its results in *numerical notation*, the *nature of its processes* must consequently be *arithmetical* and *numerical*, rather than *algebraical* and *analytical*.
>
> This is an error. The engine can arrange and combine its numerical quantities exactly as if they were *letters* or any other *general* symbols; and in fact it might bring out its results in algebraical *notation*, were provisions made accordingly.

Babbage's new Engine could do three things: process mathematical formula written in symbols, crunch numbers and calculate algebraical results in literal notation.

> It might develop three sets of results simultaneously, viz. *symbolic* results (as already alluded to in Notes A and B), *numerical* results (its chief and primary object); and *algebraical* results in *literal* notation.
>
> This latter however has not been deemed a necessary or desirable addition to its powers, partly because the necessary arrangements for effecting it would increase the complexity and extent of the mechanism to a degree that would not be commensurate with the advantages, where the main object of the invention is to translate into *numerical* language general formulæ of analysis already known to us, or whose laws of formation are known to us.
>
> Nonetheless, the production *algebraical* results in *literal* notation were only excluded from the new Engine for practical reasons. The machine was able to process all three types.
>
> But it would be a mistake to suppose that because its *results* are given in the *notation* of a more restricted science, its *processes* are therefore restricted to those of that science. The object of the engine is in fact to give the *utmost practical efficiency* to the resources of *numerical interpretations* of the higher science of analysis, while it uses the processes and combinations of this latter.

While she states what machines like the Engine may be capable of doing in the future subject to the advance of technology, she is quite clear on what the limitations of the current design are. It cannot assist directly with solving theoretical problems in mathematics. The new engine will only be able to manipulate formulas that are known to be true.

It is desirable to guard against the possibility of exaggerated ideas that might arise as to the powers of the Analytical Engine. In considering any new subject, there is frequently a tendency, first, to *overrate* what we find to be already interesting or remarkable; and, secondly, by a sort of natural reaction, to *undervalue* the true state of the case, when we do discover that our notions have surpassed those that were really tenable.

The Analytical Engine has no pretensions whatever to *originate* anything. It can do whatever we *know how to order it* to perform. It can *follow* analysis; but it has no power of *anticipating* any analytical relations or truths. Its province is to assist us in making *available* what we are already acquainted with. This it is calculated to effect primarily and chiefly of course, through its executive faculties...

Nonetheless, she speculates that using the machine in practice will generate numerical data with regularities – such as the Benouille numbers or the number pi perhaps – that will create new theoretical questions.

[B]ut it is likely to exert an *indirect* and reciprocal influence on science itself in another manner.

For, in so distributing and combining the truths and the formulæ of analysis, that they may become most easily and rapidly amenable to the mechanical combinations of the engine, the relations and the nature of many subjects in that science are necessarily thrown into new lights, and more profoundly investigated.

This is a decidedly indirect, and a somewhat *speculative*, consequence of such an invention. It is however pretty evident, on general principles, that in devising for mathematical truths a new form in which to record and throw themselves out for actual use, views are likely to be induced, which should again react on the more theoretical phase of the subject.

There are in all extensions of human power, or additions to human knowledge, various *collateral* influences, besides the main and primary object attained.

It is this last sentence that separates the intelligence of Ada and Babbage most clearly by type. Babbage had (curiously) little interest in the practical impact of his second engine. His restless energy circled mathematics and the practical technical questions that had escaped the great mathematicians Leibniz and Pascal. The question where things might end up, however, was exactly what drove Ada to support Babbage. There were other interesting and brilliant men in London society, but it was the phenomenal potential that could make Babbage's engine soar beyond any other intellectual endeavour that attracted her to him.

That did not mean that she was easily seduced by grand scientific claims the way her mother clung to new fads like a moth to a flame. It is important that the technical side of Ada's *Notes* is often very complex. The fact that this chapter quotes from her non-technical passages ought not to obscure the fact of the main thrust of the essay. The *Notes* and the translation relate almost entirely to the functioning of the machine, not its potential. It was precisely the fact that, in her own assessment, the machine could indeed do exactly what Babbage said it could that made her so interested in it and willing to devote herself to Babbage. Rare perhaps for someone who was largely self-taught rather than schooled, she was clear-sighted about the fact that good science is not about making claims but about formulating assertions that can be disproven. Building the machine would test the truth of what she had written.

> To return to the executive faculties of this engine: the question must arise in every mind, are they *really* even able to *follow* analysis in its whole extent? No reply, entirely satisfactory to all minds, can be given to this query, excepting the actual existence of the engine, and actual experience of its practical results.

It took Ada to see what the Analytical Engine truly represented in the forward evolution of human technology. It took Ada to realise that the Jacquard loom provided the first example in the history of human technology of the process of digitisation of daily life and not just mathematics, a process that the Analytical Engine was furthering. Ada realised that the Analytical Engine could be applied to *any* process involving the manipulation of information. She saw and wrote that it heralded the birth of a new science, the science of digitising information, one that went well beyond Babbage's vision, or the imagination of those around her.

It was a science that tantalisingly might easily have been born in the middle of the nineteenth century Britain rather than a hundred years later.

In the final stanza of the third canto of *Childe Harold's Pilgrimage*, Byron describes Ada as

> The child of love, though born in bitterness,
>   And nurtured in convulsion.

Ada's character may have suffered from those convulsions in the same way that Babbage's was affected by a life bathed in praise, but her mind had not. Where science was concerned it was as sharp as Ockham's razor.

15

𝒜da's 𝒪ffer to ℬabbage

Ada and Babbage met on several occasions during the spring and summer of 1843, a time they seem to have thought of each other as kindred spirits. It is known that Ada got Babbage to check over the proofs of the *Notes*.

Babbage says in his autobiography that he offered to do part of the work on the *Notes* 'to save Lady Lovelace the trouble'.

This part of Ada's *Notes* is 'Note G' dealing with the Bernoulli numbers (in his autobiography, Babbage misspells the name as 'Bernouilli'). Bernoulli numbers themselves are a sequence of rational numbers that are extremely important in various areas of number theory.

Note G is especially relevant to us today. It describes step by step, in detail, the 'operations' through which the punched cards would proceed to weave an even longer sequence of Bernoulli numbers on the Analytical Engine. Note G is highly complex, juggling mathematics and technology. Most importantly of all, it is in effect a program containing instructions for a computer. Even though the Analytical Engine has not so far been built, and the effectiveness of the program cannot be tested until one is, Note G is considered by some to be the first computer program ever written.

The question therefore arises: who can claim the credit of being the first computer programmer? In his memoir Babbage writes that he had 'offered to do [G] to save Lady Lovelace the trouble.' But he concedes that she corrected 'a grave mistake which I had made in the process'.

As it happens Ada's correspondence relating to Note G was saved from destruction (by her mother Lady Byron, perhaps). There are two letters on successive days that are particularly interesting. Ada wrote to Babbage on Tuesday July 4 and Wednesday July 5 1843. She had been ill, and it is obvious that her hard work on Babbage's behalf was making her feel better. She writes respectfully to her friend:

Tuesday Morning, Ockham

My Dear Babbage

I now write to you expressly on *three* points; which I have very fully & leisurely considered during the last 18 hours; & think of sufficient importance to induce me to send a servant up so that you may have this letter by half after six this evening. The servant will leave Town tomorrow morning early, but will call for anything you may have for me, at *eight* o'clock in the morning before he goes.

Firstly: the few lines I enclosed you last night about the connexion of (8) with the famous Integral, I by no means intend you to insert, unless you *fully* approve the doing so.

It is perhaps very dubious whether there is any sufficient *pertinence* in noticing *at all* that (8) is an *Integral*...

Secondly: Lord L – suggests my *signing* the translation & the Notes; by which he means, simply putting at the end of the former: *'translated by A.A.L.;'* & adding to each note the initials A.A.L.

As if working on a medieval cathedral, Ada appears not to have even thought of putting her name to her *Notes* and the translation and it was only upon the prompting of Lord Lovelace – for the time being a mathematics widower – that she thought of putting this forward.

However, on the actual topic of the article she had no reserve and was nothing but forthright, describing Note G as a 'mess', not the attribute of a successful computer programme running by necessity from logical step. In the description 'mess' one recognises the fertile, gnomic, quixotic and dilettante mind of Babbage himself when attempting to convey his views to third parties such as Robert Peel, Mary Somerville or even his friend Lyell.

My third topic, tho' my last, is our most anxious & important:-

I have yesterday evening & this morning very amply analysed the question of the *number* of Variable-Cards, as mentioned in the final Note H (or G?). And I find that you & I between us have made a *mess* of it; (for which I can perfectly account, in a very natural manner). I enclose what I wish to insert *instead* of that which is now there. I think the present *wrong* passage is only about eight or ten lines, & is I believe on the *second* of the three great sheets which are to *follow* the Diagram...

I can scarcely describe to you how *very* ill & harassed I felt yesterday. Pray excuse any abruptness or other unpleasantness of manner, if there were any.

I am breathing *well* again today, & am much better in all respects; owing to Dr L's remedies. He certainly does seem to understand the case, I mean the *treatment* of it, which is the main thing.

As for the *theory* of it, he says truly that *time* & *Providence* alone can develop that. It is so *anomalous* an affair altogether. A *Singular Function*, in very deed!

Think of my having to *walk* (or rather *run*) to the Station, in *half an hour* last evening; while I suppose *you* were feasting & flirting in luxury & ease at your dinner. It must be a very pleasant merry sort of thing to have a *Fairy* in one's service, mind & limbs! – I envy you! – *I*, poor little Fairy, can only get dull heavy *mortals*, to wait on *me*! –

Ever Yours

A.L.

The next day she corrects the order of cards further in no uncertain terms.

Wednesday, 5 July, Ockham Park
My Dear Babbage
I am much obliged by the contents of your letter, in all respects. Should you find it expedient to substitute the amended passage about the Variable-Cards, there is also *one* other *short* sentence which must be altered similarly. This sentence precedes the passage I sent yesterday by perhaps half a page or more. It is where I explain that for every B after B_5, operations (13 … .23) have to be repeated; & I believe it runs as follows:
'Not only are the *Operation* Cards precisely the same for the repetition, but the Variable Cards as well with the exception of one new one to introduce B5 instead of Bs for operation 21 to act upon.'
I should wish to substitute what I enclose.

Babbage's response to her is not known, and probably lost forever.

But in the same letter she mentions an allusion by him to the 'imaginary roots' of their friendship in his response. Oblique as to what exactly the joke is, his words make her puzzle for their meaning and she settles on the word 'Fairy' to whom she had compared herself as his helper. It was a word with which she liked to describe herself to others around this time of her marriage. Flirtatiously she only half jokes to him that what she will do in the next ten years will be eternal rather than die with her.

'Why does my friend prefer *imaginary* roots for our friendship?' – Just because she happens to have some of that very imagination which *you* would deny her to possess; & therefore she enjoys a little *play* & *scope* for it now & then. Besides this, I deny the *Fairyism* to be entirely *imaginary*; (& it is to the *fairy* similes that I suppose you allude).
That *brain* of mine is something more than merely *mortal*, as time will show; (if only my *breathing* & some other et-ceteras do not make too rapid a progress *towards* instead of *from* mortality).-
Before ten years are over, the Devil's in it if I have not sucked out some of the life-blood from the mysteries of this universe, in a way that no purely mortal lips or brains could do.
No one knows what almost *awful* energy & power lie yet undeveloped in that *wiry* little system of mine. I say *awful*, because you may imagine that it *might* be under certain circumstances.

Then it is business as usual and she instructs Babbage when she would like him to be available if she has any questions about the Bernoulli numbers she is 'doggedly attacking and sifting to the very bottom'.

> I do not go to Town until Monday. Keep yourself open if you can for that day; in case there should be anything I wish to see you about, which is very likely. But the *evening* I think is most likely to be my time for you, as I rather expect to be engaged incessantly until after 6 o'clock.
>
> I shall sleep in Town that night.-
>
> I am doggedly attacking & sifting to the very bottom, all the ways of deducing the Bernoulli Numbers. In the manner I am grappling with this subject, & connecting it with others, I shall be some days upon it.
>
> I shall then take in succession the *other* subjects that have been suggested to me during my late labours, & treat them similarly.-
>
> '*Labor ipse voluptas*' is in *very* deed my motto! – And, (as I hinted just now), it is perhaps well for the world that my line & ambition is over the *spiritual*; & that I have not taken it into my head, or lived in times & circumstances calculated to put it into my head, to deal with the sword, poison, & intrigue, in the place of x, y, & z.
>
> By the way I shall set to work upon *Ohm* tomorrow, & continue it daily until I finish it.
>
> Your *Fairy* for ever
>
> A.A.L.

Ada's insights into Babbage's work were not just confined to her understanding of what the Analytical Engine really was. She also understood Babbage and, for all her affection and admiration for him, she knew that if his dreams were to come true, he needed help. And that was why, on August 15 1843, she wrote one of the most poignant letters in the history of the computer. It is also one of the longest. Covering sixteen pages of her close handwriting, it runs to more than 2,000 words.

If there is a moment in Ada's story when we reach a crossroads where the future of the computer was at stake, this letter provides that moment. Ada's letter to Babbage constituted an offer to handle, henceforth, what would be regarded today as the management, political and public relations aspects of Babbage's work on the Analytical Engine. Ada admired Babbage but she was certain that the ornery and undiplomatic aspects of his personality greatly handicapped him when it came to advancing the cause of his Engines.

Ada was perceptive enough to understand something that Babbage never saw: that advancing his project required not only technical wizardry but also needed a velvet yet driven skill at dealing with influential and skeptical people.

He and Ada sometimes had rifts with each other, and this letter shows Ada trying to mend one.

My Dear Babbage

You would have heard from me several days ago, but for the *hot* work that has been going on between me & the printers. This is now happily concluded. I have endeavoured to work up everything to the utmost perfection, *as far as it goes;* & I am now well satisfied on the whole, since I think that *within the sphere of views* I set out with, & in accordance with which the whole contents & arrangement of the Notes are shaped, they are very complete, & even admirable. I could *now* do the thing *far better*; but this would be from setting out upon a wholly different *basis*.

I say you would have heard from me before. Your note (enclosed on Monday with my papers & c), is such as demands a very full reply from me, the writer being so old & so esteemed a friend, *& one whose genius I not only so highly appreciate myself, but wish to see fairly appreciated by others.*

Were it not for this desire (which both Lord L – & myself have more warmly at heart than you are as yet at all aware of), coupled with our long-established regard & intercourse, I should say that *the less notice taken by me of that note – the better*, & it was only worthy to be thrown aside with a smile of contempt. The *tone* of it, it is impossible to misunderstand; & as I am myself always a very *'explicit function of x'*, I shall not pretend to do so; & shall leave to *you* (if you please it) to continue the *'implicit'* style which is exceedingly marked in the said note.

As I know you will not be *explicit* enough to state the *real* state of your feelings respecting me at this time, I shall do so for you. You feel, my dear Babbage, that *I* have (tho' in a negative manner) *added* to the list of injuries & of disappointments & mis-comprehensions that you have already experienced in a life by no means smooth or fortunate. You *know* this is your feeling; & that you are deeply hurt about it; & you endeavour to derive a poor & sorry consolation from such sentiments as 'Well, she didn't *know* or *intend* the injury & mischief if she has done' &c....

I must now come to a practical question respecting the future. *Your* affairs have been, & are, deeply occupying both myself & Lord Lovelace. Our thoughts as well as our conversation have been earnest upon them. And the result is that I have plans for you, which I do not think fit at present to communicate to you; but which I shall either develop, or else throw my energies, my time & pen into the service of some other department of truth & science, according to the reply I receive from you to what I am now going to state. I do beseech you therefore deeply & seriously to ponder over the question how far you can subscribe to my conditions or not. I give to *you* the *first* choice & offer of my services & my intellect. Do not lightly reject them. I say this entirely for *your own* sake, believe me.

My channels for developing [sic] & training my scientific & literary powers, are various, & some of them very attractive. But I wish my old friend to have the *refusal*.

Firstly: I want to know whether if I continue to work *on* & *about* your own great subject, you will undertake to abide wholly by the judgement of myself (or of any persons whom you may *now* please to name as referees, whenever we may differ), on *all practical* matters relating to *whatever can involve relations with any fellow-creature or fellow-creatures*.

Secondly: can you undertake to give your mind *wholly* & *undividedly*, as a primary object that no engagement is to interfere with, to the consideration of all those matters in which I shall at times require your intellectual *assistance* & *supervision*; & can you promise not to *slur* & *hurry* things over; or to mislay, & allow confusion & mistakes to enter into documents, &c?

Thirdly: If I am able to lay before you in the course of a year or two, explicit & honorable propositions for *executing your engine*, (such as are approved by persons whom you may *now* name to be referred to for their approbation), would there be any chance of your allowing myself & such parties to conduct the business for you; your own *undivided* energies being devoted to the execution of the work; & all other matters being arranged for you on terms which your *own* friends should approve?

You will wonder over this last query. But, I strongly advise you not to reject it as chimerical. You do *not* know the grounds I have for believing that such a contingency may come within my power, & I wish to know before I allow my mind to employ its energies any further on the subject, that I shall not be wasting thought & power for no purpose or result....

Yours is to love truth & God (yes, deeply & constantly); but to love *fame, glory, honours, yet more*. You will deny this; but in all your intercourse with *every* human being (as far as I know & see of it), it is a *practically paramount* sentiment. Mind, I am not *blaming* it. I simply state my belief in the *fact*. The fact may be a very *noble & beautiful* fact. *That* is another question.

Will you come *here* for some days on Monday. I hope so. Lord L – is very anxious to see & converse with you; & was vexed that the Rail called him away on Tuesday before he had heard from yourself your own views about the recent affair.

I sadly want your *Calculus of Functions*. So *Pray* get it for me. I cannot understand the *Examples*.

I have ventured inserting to one passage of Note G a small Foot-Note, which I am sure is *quite tenable*. I say in it that the engine is remarkably well adapted to include the *whole Calculus of Finite Differences*, & I allude to the computation of the *Bernoullian Numbers by means of the difference of Nothing*, as a beautiful example for its processes. I hope it *is* correctly the case.

This letter is sadly blotted & corrected. Never mind that however.

I wonder if you will choose to retain the lady-fairy in your service or not.

Yours ever most sincerely.

A.A.L

*

Babbage didn't accept the offer. He didn't realise just how brilliant her understanding of his work really was, still less how deep her understanding of his personality was. One wonders how intently he had even read the discursive part of her *Notes*. If he had read them properly, wouldn't he have realised just how useful her insights were into the advancement of the Analytical Engine?

There is no written evidence surviving that Babbage truly understood what Ada had written about the Analytical Engine. In reading her *Notes*, he may have focused merely on the complex mathematical material (and attributed – or blamed – what he saw as its more discursive ideas on her 'fairy' imagination).

All we know is that the day after Ada wrote this letter, Babbage said no to her without much consideration. At the top of the long letter that Ada sent him on August 14 and which is to be found in the Babbage papers, there appears a pencilled note in Babbage's hand stating, simply:

Tuesday 15 saw AAL this morning and refused all the conditions.

Babbage could on occasion be selfish, stubborn and ungenerous of spirit where his work was concerned. In that short note he combines all three vices. Despite his respect for Ada's ability to articulate and popularise the most important project of his life, he could never see her as anything more than an 'interpreter'. Ada's reaction to what he told her on Tuesday, or, indeed, how exactly he told her what he had decided is not recorded.

Ada's translation of Menabrea's paper on the Analytical Engine was published a few days later in September 1843 in the third number of *Scientific Memoirs*. Entitled *Sketch of the Analytical Engine invented by Charles Babbage, Esq. (by L. F. Menabrea, with notes by Ada Lovelace)*. It was respectfully received by the scientific and mathematical community, but did not cause the sensation Babbage no doubt hoped for, nor did it prove to be the springboard to a literary and scientific career for Ada.

One of the big problems was that Ada was a woman, and although she had signed her *Notes* only with the initials A.A.L., her authorship soon became generally known. The very fact that she was a woman ended up working against her, because the scientific community did not take her work seriously, as it would have done if she had been a man.

16

The Enchantress of Number

If Ada was upset with Babbage, and surely she must have felt some disappointment that her idea had been dismissed, this is not apparent from her or his letters that survive from after her proposal to him

Nonetheless, there are no surviving letters from Ada to Babbage between the long one she wrote on August 14 1843 and a short one she wrote to him on March 4 1845. Instead, we have a letter from Babbage to her, which he wrote on September 9 1843, that opens a casual window on the nature of their relationship.

This is not the first surviving letter after August 14 1843; there is another, shorter letter, on August 18 1843 about some drawings he had sent her, and concerning some mathematical papers that she had apparently asked him about, though it's not clear whether she asked him verbally or in a letter.

That day was clearly a day when Babbage was desperately frustrated with his life and with the difficulties he was facing in his work. He decided to put all the miseries of London behind him, and went to see Ada and her husband – though it was clearly Ada he most wanted to see – at their home at Ashley Combe. Rather than hunting, riding, shooting or other leisurely country house pursuits, he was planning to take the train up to Ashley Combe to tackle with Ada topics of cutting-edge mathematics that had recently been discovered.

My Dear Lady Lovelace
I find it quite in vain to wait until I have leisure so I have resolved that I will leave all other things undone and set out for Ashley taking with me papers enough to enable me to forget this world and all its troubles and if possible its multitudinous Charlatans – everything in short but the Enchantress of Number.

My only impediment would be my mother's health which is not at this moment quite so good as I could wish.

Are you at Ashley? And is it still consistent with all your other arrangements that I should join you there? – and will next Wednesday or next Thursday or any other day suit you: and shall I leave the iron-shod road at Thornton or at Bridgewater and have you got Arbogast *Du Calcul des derivations* with you there (i.e. at Ashley). I shall bring some books about that horrible problem – the three bodies which is almost as obscure as the existence of the celebrated book *De Tribu Impostoribus* so if you have Arbogast I will bring something else.

Farewell my dear and much admired Interpreter.
Evermost Truly Yours
Charles Babbage

Louis Arbogast's *Du Calcul des derivations* was published in 1800 and contains the statement of a formula that would only receive widespread recognition 55 years later when it was named after an Italian mathematician, Faà di Bruno, who published two versions of the formula in an Italian academic journal. Not surprisingly, in 1834 the mathematical problem was still so new and difficult that Babbage refers to jokingly it as *De Tribu Impostoribus*. The educated would recognise the name as the mythical book that denied all three Abrahamic religions: Christianity, Judaism and Islam. It was a common rumour from the eleventh century to the eighteenth century that there was a heretical text by this name, but it never existed. Ossian-style, in France and Germany two hoaxes were published under its name (as the power of religion wilted from the nineteenth century onwards, however, so would the rumour).

What is, furthermore, curious about this letter is the use of the phrase 'Enchantress of Number' for Ada. Babbage wrote 'Number' in the singular. This point needs making because there is a comprehensive misconception that he wrote 'Enchantress of Numbers' in the plural. A search for the phrase 'Enchantress of Numbers' on Google reveals 390,000 references, all wrong.

However the word 'Number' in the singular is unmistakably there at the end of the page of the manuscript of the letter. The mark to the right of the word is clearly a full stop.

What did Babbage mean by 'Enchantress of Number'? The modern answer might be that he simply misspelled the word. However, such a slip of the pen seems unusual in a time where good spelling was – unlike now, perhaps – generally considered a sign of distinction.

The other obvious suggestion is that he meant to describe Ada as an enchantress. There is sense in this as Dr Johnson defines a fairy in his 1755 Dictionary as an 'enchantress, an elf, a fay', and to Babbage Ada described herself as a fairy during this period. But there is a social difference. Few would thoughtlessly repeat a joke that a correspondent has just made about themselves. Dr Johnson defines the word 'enchantress' itself less innocently as 'a sorceress; a woman of extreme beauty or excellence', and a 'sorceress' as a 'female magician or enchantress.' Ada had never been encouraged to believe she was exceptionally gifted, let alone think of herself as an exceptional beauty. Whatever she may have felt deep inside, these views hadn't changed in the August letter she had written to Babbage. The almost camp hyperbole of the word enchantress as a way of describing her powers might have made someone like Ada feel ill at ease, if indeed Babbage had meant to flatter her by way of a joke.

The Babbage who speaks through his letters or emerges from the books about his life does not seem someone who would so expressly refer to Ada herself in the direct, flirtatious if not seductive tone that a poet like Lord Byron might permit himself when writing to a married noblewoman whose husband's country house he would like to visit. That is a different matter from the Babbage who, to others such as Michael Faraday, refers flatteringly to Ada as an 'Enchantress who has thrown her magical spell around the most abstract of Sciences and has grasped it with a force which few masculine intellects (in our own country at least) could have exerted over it.'

If it is not Ada, the enchantress is either the Analytical Engine or mathematics itself. Given their close working relationship on Menabrea's essay at this time and Babbage's monomaniacal obsession with the new machine, it is more likely that he meant the former. Ada's and Babbage's correspondence is functional and not, ultimately, that of equals, as Babbage had made clear in August. The clue lies perhaps in his complaint to Ada, 'I find it quite in vain to wait until I have leisure…', and he will come to Ashley but 'leave all other things undone'. At Ada's he will devote himself exclusively to his work, leaving behind the 'world and all its troubles.'

He leavens this heavy-handed lament with light-hearted kennings: the railway becomes the 'iron-shod road', an essential book on mathematical series that will be worked on by the two becomes a mythical religious tome. In fact, Arbogast's book was far from 'mythical'. The book developed an idea that was crucial to the success of the engine. Arbogast writes in the prelims to his book, 'The secret power of Analysis consists in the happy choice and application of signs, which are simple and characteristic of the things they represent.' Thus the light-hearted circumlocution for an engine that would handle infinite fractions and formulas accurately became the 'enchantress': not of numbers in plural, but of the analytical concept itself.

So by 'Enchantress of Number' Babbage appears to have meant the Analytical Engine. The possibility that he was writing in an obfuscated spirit of flirtation and did mean Ada, and she read it as such, is tantalising. But if it was amorous it seems curious that he repeated it casually to Faraday. Without the discovery of any conclusive evidence it is not clear that their relationship was 'impure' in Lord Byron's terms.

The letter makes clear that Ada had taken being rebuffed by Babbage very well indeed. It had not dented her resolve to help the gestation of the Analytical Engine in any way she could as a 'fairy'. She was not serving mere mortals but the Enchantress herself. No wonder Babbage signed off warmly to the only one in the world who gave him unconditional help, despite all, and who saw the significance of what he was trying to achieve.

Apart from Ada, there was one man in the nineteenth century who grasped, in its technical detail at least, the exceptional value of Babbage's work. Federico Luigi Menabrea was a professor of engineering at the University of Turin when he wrote his essay on Babbage that Ada translated (he thought she was called 'Lady Lovely'). Originally an army engineer before he became a professor, he would become involved in politics in the mid-1840s and enter the Italian cabinet in 1861 as navy minister.

Menabrea's rise to prominence at that time may well have been an important factor for Babbage to publish his memoir *Passages from the Life of a Philosopher* in 1864. Menabrea's name was now commonly known in Britain's government circles. However, whatever the demands of the Italian navy, the fiendishly complicated cogwheels of Italian unification now absorbed Menabrea (he was to become Italian prime minister a few years later in 1867). There was little he could do personally – even if he had remembered his essay and wanted to use his position to advance Babbage's now somewhat stale project.

Thus the year 1864 was marked in the UK by the publication of Babbage's *Passages*. But also by a biting satire of the Engine together with a portrait of his odd, self-aggrandising pettiness in Charles Dickens' *All the Year Round*, showing the inventor to be relentlessly bullied by his neighbours who knew they could get a rise out of him simply by making noise in front of his house:

Some of Mr Babbage's neighbours have derived great pleasure from inviting musicians of various tastes and countries to play opposite his house, with the view of ascertaining whether there are not some kinds of instruments which he might approve; but their best efforts have had no other effect than to bring the philosopher out into the street in search of a policeman.

What a misfortune it is to a man to have no taste for music! There goes Mr Babbage in search of an officer of the law followed by a crowd of young children, urged on by their parents and backed at a judicious distance by a set of vagabonds shouting forth uncomplimentary epithets, and making ridiculous rhymes on his name. When he turns round to survey his illustrious tail, it stops; if he moves towards it, it recedes; but, the instant he turns, the shouting and the abuse are resumed. In one case there were above a hundred persons, consisting of men, women, and boys, who followed him through the streets before he could find a policeman…

A foolish young fellow purchased a wind instrument with a hole in it, with which he made discordant noises for the purpose of annoying him. A workman inhabiting an attic which overlooked his garden, blew a penny whistle out of his window every day for half an hour. When Mr Babbage took measures to put a stop to these proceedings he was threatened with vengeance. One correspondent kindly volunteered to do him a serious bodily injury, while a third, in a personal communication, intimated his intention of burning the house down with Mr Babbage in it. The smaller evils of dead cats thrown down his area, of windows from time to time purposely broken, or of occasional blows on the head from stones projected by unseen hands, Mr Babbage will not condescend to speak.

All these things are trifles compared to being awakened at one o'clock in the morning (just as he has fallen asleep after a painful surgical operation) by the crash of a brass band. On a careful retrospect of the last dozen years of his life, Mr Babbage arrives at the conclusion that one-fourth part of his working power has been destroyed by street music which he regards as a twenty-five per cent income-tax on his brain, levied by permission of the government, and squandered among the most worthless classes. During eighty days he registered one hundred and sixty-five instances when he went out to put a stop to the nuisance. In several of these instances his whole day's work was lost, for they frequently occurred when he was giving instructions to his workmen relative to some parts of his analytical engine.

At the end of his life, Babbage truly had become the charicature of a mad scientist – even to his former friend.

17

A Horrible Death

After 1843, the most intellectually exciting year of Ada's life, she continued (not always explicably) to be friends with Babbage and having quite a busy social life among the higher echelons of Victorian intellectual society, her friends including Charles Dickens, Michael Faraday and many other literary and scientific luminaries of the age.

Her mother was also busy with her social life and with her various health preoccupations. It is possible that Ada met Countess Teresa Guiccioli, Byron's former lover, who was travelling with her new husband, the Marquis of Boissy, and spent some time in London with him. The Marquis had pursued Teresa ardently before she succumbed to him, and he was always deeply proud that she had been Byron's lover. Boissy liked to introduce Teresa to people as 'Madame la Marquise de Boissy, autrefois la Maitresse de Milord Byron' (Madam the Marchioness of Boissy, formerly the mistress of Lord Byron).

Teresa lived into old age. She survived until 1873 and so outlived not only Lord Byron and his only legitimate daughter, but also Lady Byron and Babbage.

Babbage most likely met the Countess and, while Lady Byron would naturally not have been keen for Ada to meet Teresa, Ada possibly did. Teresa evidently liked London and visited there on more than one occasion. Teresa was interested in science and attended at least one lecture, in 1845, given by the well-known scientific populariser Dionysius Lardner, whose lectures Ada herself had attended avidly ten years earlier to understand the Difference Engine. The actor William Macready, who was probably the person who introduced Babbage to Dickens and vice versa, wrote in his diary on June 18 1835 that he had gone to Dr Lardner's house and met, among other people, Teresa Guiccioli.

Ada wrote two letters to Babbage in 1844, asking him what to do about someone Ada seems to have called 'Countess Italia-Italia', though the transcription is hard to be sure about. However, Babbage had probably met Teresa himself during one of her visits to London, and it is at least possible that Ada met her herself, but there is no definite evidence for this.

Much of Ada's life during her last years is inadequately documented. It is known that she became interested in the late 1840s in horse-racing, and became quite addicted to this pursuit and lost large sums of money on gambling, at the beginning of 1850 apparently, when slips of paper with tips addressed to her maid can be found among her papers. According to her son Ralph, she lost about £3200 on betting on horse races; this was a vast sum at the time and it is not clear how Ada paid it. She suffered almost continual money problems in the last few years of her life. William could not help her much as he himself had times when he was short of cash and was in any case parsimonious, and Lady Byron, while on occasion generous to Ada and in possession of a vast fortune, did not regularly help Ada financially.

There have been some efforts to investigate whether she might have been trying to develop, perhaps with Babbage's help, some kind of mathematical system for betting on horses. These efforts are spurred on by Ada and Babbage mentioning a 'book' (it is not known what kind of book they mean) in letters in 1848 and 1849. It has been speculated that the word referred to a book, a term used in horseracing. But it is more likely that it referred to a book that they perhaps planned to write together to continue their cooperation over the *Notes*. This illusory project would have provided Babbage with a face-saving way to maintain their friendship and avoid having to give Ada a blunt 'no' to her long written request of being involved with the Engine after the *Notes*.

On September 7 1850, not long before her death, Ada finally visited Newstead Abbey for the first and last time in her life. She was travelling with her husband William in the north of England and visited the Abbey, as well as the popular novelists Edward Bulwer Lytton and Walter Scott, and the owners of a racehorse she had mentioned to Lady Byron. Ada and William's host was Colonel Wildman, who had been busily restoring Newstead Abbey after having bought it from Lord Byron. Lady Byron had herself made a visit to Newstead Abbey, alone without Ada, in 1818, and had written a feeble poem about being there:

I remember when beside the bed
Which pillowed last that too reposeless head,
I stood – so undesert'd looked the scene
As there at eve its inhabitants had been.
Struck by that thought, and rooted to the ground,
Instinctively I listen'd, look'd around,
Whilst banish'd passion rushed to claim again
Its throne, all vacant in my breast till then.
And pardon'd be the wish, when thus deceiv'd
To perish, ere of hope again bereav'd!

Ada, for her part, was profoundly moved by her own visit to Newstead Abbey. After she and William arrived, Colonel Wildman gave them a tour of the main chambers, and they were then shown to their rooms, which were above the old cloister, overlooking the Gothic fountain. Ada and William appear to have had separate rooms at Newstead.

Ada's initial response to Newstead Abbey was that Wildman had done an excellent job of the renovations and spent money such as 'no Byron could have afforded', but that the place seemed bereft of the spirit of her father. On September 8 she wrote gloomily to her mother that she felt:

[L]ow and melancholy. All is like death round one; & I seem to be in the Mausoleum of my race. What is the good of living, when thus all passes away & leaves only cold stone behind it? There is no life here, but cold dreary death only... I am glad to see the home of my ancestors but I shall not be sorry to escape from the grave. I see my own future continuing visibly around me... I have not yet seen my father's rooms. No one is here but the Hamilton Greys, & we are perfectly quiet, & just like Goody Two Shoes!

Only I feel as if I had become a stone monument myself. I am petrifying fast.

However, on September 10, when Ada went for a walk by herself in the grounds of the abbey, she wandered among places such as the Devil's Wood, a thick, dark grove of trees overlooking one of the fishponds. Walking in the grounds, Ada was haunted by feelings about the father she had never seen. Colonel Wildman encountered her there in the grounds, and while it is not clear what she and Wildman spoke about, it appears that she told him much about her feelings about her father, his Cambridge friend.

On this meeting, Julian Hawthorn recounts in the biography of his father Nathaniel a letter from his mother in which she describes what her landlady at Newstead had told her during their visit to Byron's former home. Wildman had invited Ada to Newstead, expecting a 'pleasant knowledgeable guest' and he had read up on his classics and mathematics to be well prepared for his well-read guest. Instead the Ada who turned up was 'not beautiful, and did not resemble her father at all', she was 'extremely careless in her dress... very silent and gloomy.' Fed up after two days of 'Yes' and 'No' to questions, Colonel Wildman finally followed her into the garden and 'accosted her with resolute sociability.' Under his friendly attack Ada's sepulchral mood finally broke down. She explained why she was so glum and the rest of the visit she was indeed the delightful guest he had hoped for.

The experience Ada had at Newstead Abbey led to a rift between Ada and Lady Byron that probably never completely healed. Ada had received money before the trip from her, on this rare occasion, munificent mother. But neither she nor William were subsequently able to conceal the emotional closeness she had felt to her father while at Newstead, and Lady Byron became convinced that Ada was now taking the long-dead Byron's side against Lady Byron's, which it appears Ada was indeed doing. There is evidence that after visiting Newstead Abbey, Ada was never again as close to her mother as she, Ada, had been before going there.

Her friendship with Babbage continued to be an important part of her life and his.

In an undated letter Babbage sent her that was most likely written in 1851, Babbage even felt able to confide in Ada, rather self-pityingly but also movingly, about his loneliness. At the time, it was usual for wives whose husbands had left the marital home to place advertisements in newspapers offering forgiveness and reconciliation if the husbands would come home. In those days before the telephone and long before the internet, this was just about the only technique available to communicate to the 'wandering lords', as Babbage described them. The husbands were, naturally, not referred to in the advertisements by their names but by initials.

Colonel Thomas Wildman, 1831 (Thomas Lawrence).

Babbage, seeing some of these advertisements one day, was seized with a consciousness of his own loneliness.

My dear Lady Lovelace
I sat last night reading the advertisements of deserted wifes to charm back their wandering lords.
    I am not a wanderer though I had none to charm me...

Another glimpse of how he feels inwardly is provided by Babbage including on the title page of his autobiography the lines *'I'm a philosopher. Confound them all! / Birds, beasts and men; but – no, not womankind'* which appear in Byron's long poem *Don Juan*.

The lines are at the start of Canto Six, stanza 22, but Babbage has misquoted the passage, which actually reads as *I'm a philosopher; confound them all -/ Bills, beasts and men; and – no, not womankind!'*

But even though Babbage thought Byron had written 'birds' when he meant 'bills' (logical enough things for Byron to object to), the emphasis on a belief in womankind being the salvation is what really matters here, and Babbage obviously shares this belief.

Here, as in the reference to the wandering lords and in the letter where he may be describing Ada as the Enchantress of Number, we encounter sudden depths opening up that give us peeks into the deeply-feeling and even romantic man who seems much of the rest of the time to have kept this aspect of his personality in check.

The misquotation may be due to Babbage confusing the lines in *Don Juan* with an extract from Byron's poem *Darkness*, which reads:

… and kept
The birds and beasts and famish'd men at bay.

Did Babbage and Ada ever read Byron's poetry together? It is a tantalising idea, but there is no record that they did. What they did most likely do is have many walks together discussing subjects that surely included mathematics, philosophy, Babbage's Engines and – perhaps – poetry. Part of the terrace at Ada's country home Ashley in Somerset became known as 'Philosopher's Walk', as it was there that Ada and Babbage were reputed to have walked while having their discussions.

By the summer of 1851 Ada's health was beginning to take a serious turn for the worse. She had never been very strong during her life, and the mid to late 1840s had been a period for her of intermittent illness, and she often suffered from nervous exhaustion and general debilitation almost as a matter of course. By the summer of 1851, however, Ada began to suffer from the first signs of uterine cancer. This initially manifested itself in frequent bleeding which, to start with, was painless. Ada knew she was not well, but at first she remained optimistic. On July 24 1851 she wrote to her husband William:

Now as to my health: I do not agree with you that the progress is *slow*. When we consider that I have *not* been quite *2 months* under treatment, for a most serious complaint which had existed (more or less) for upward of a year, – I think we cannot call the present state other than *very* satisfactory. Not only is there an improvement in *nerves* & in general health which is obvious to everyone, & is most of all felt & known to myself – but the *local* condition is no longer *vicious*. Dr Locock explained to me yesterday how threatening & how morbid it *had* been.

He said that tho' now there is still an extense deep seated *sore*, yet it is a *healthy* sore.

Within a month she started feeling less positive about things (the 'healthy sore' would turn out to be malignant), as in this letter she wrote again to her mother on Saturday August 16 1851:

By the bye, Dr Cape said last time, that my complaint, such as it *was*, must have injured my *mind*, & greatly impaired its power & its clearness; because that for *months previous*, there had been as it were a continuous *current drawn off* from the Brain. I often feel great *confusion* & difficulty in *concentrating my ideas*; & also if I could only *perceive one* idea at a time. At other times I felt also as if I were *dulled* & *indifferent*.

He tells me that death would have been by *total* failure of *mind*; in short the successive *fading* first of everything *human*, & then everything *vital!* Give me a *spasm* to kill me *at once*, sooner than such a dreadful fate…

But what a dreadful fate is an insidious painless disease, that undermines before one knows it.

On October 15 1851, Ada wrote to her mother:

I have been very unwell, & am getting better again; But still everything seems difficult & troublesome … But I do dread that horrible *struggle*, which I fear is in the Byron blood. I don't think we die easy. I should like to 'drop' off, gently, but quickly, some 30 or 40 years hence.

Ada would of course have been only too aware that in a few months she was about the reach the age of Lord Byron when he died. Yet despite that letter she had written to her mother, Ada tried to remain positive. Writing to her son Byron, Lord Ockham, on the same day when she wrote the just-quoted letter to her mother, Ada pens a letter that has a calm and affectionate maternal tone and gives no indication of how ill she knows she is. Presumably she wanted to keep the truth from Byron. She wrote the letter on Great Exhibition stationery. Byron was in the navy, aboard the ship *HMS Daphne*. Ada missed him a great deal. By all accounts Byron, unlike his grandfather, was not much of a letter-writer.

Dear Byron, This day has closed our Great National Exposition after a career of glory & success unequalled almost in the history of human enterprise.

We have seen one or two newspaper notices of the Daphne having gone to Vancouver's Island, but we have not heard from you now for many months…

We have heard (thro' officers of the *Champion*) that you were very well thought of there; & you were mentioned as a '*heaven-born sailor*'.

Pray continue yr heavenly career.

Most Affectly yrs

A.A. Lovelace

Ada underlines in this letter the name of the ship the *Champion* but not the *Daphne*, perhaps because it was a less familiar ship to Byron than the one he was sailing on.

Ada went with Babbage to the Great Exhibition, which took place at the Crystal Palace in Hyde Park in London, from May 1 to October 15 1851. It was, at the time, the greatest exhibition of culture and industry that had taken place in history, and it was immensely popular and hugely profitable. It started a trend in such exhibitions that lasted for about a century. There was, for example, an *Exposition universelle* held in Paris in 1855 and four more during the nineteenth century.

The unclear references she often makes in her letters to her state of mind may reflect the fact that in order to get relief from her physical pains, she often took laudanum – a powerful combination of opium and brandy – whenever she felt unwell. This drug definitely had on occasion a negative effect on her mental state, and she may have written some letters under its influence. This has led certain uncharitable commentators to suggest that she went mad or was regularly intoxicated.

Her ill-health persisted. She wrote to her son Byron from her London home at 6 Great Cumberland Place on Saturday November 15 1851, this time not leaving him under any illusions about her condition, though she starts the letter by reminding him that 'we have not heard from you for very many months'.

My health is at present very delicate and infirm, & I am obliged to be chiefly in Town; for surgical advice, & to lie up on the sofa almost entirely.

Slowly but surely and inexorably, the cancer took hold of her, causing her at first intermittent pain, then gradually worse and worse pain. For example, in a letter Ada wrote to her mother on Tuesday December 30 1851, Ada wrote:

I am going on well, excepting that I had an *awful* night from pain. I am now obliged to give up sleeping in bed altogether, & *to be dressed*, & lie on a sofa or else *outside* my bed. In this way, I get *intervals* of sleep, from being able to rise & to move about freely, without risk of catching cold. I am going on perfectly well. It is *expected* there will be a great deal of trouble from pain.

By the end of the year 1851, though, there was really nothing about Ada's health that she could be optimistic about. The pain from her cancer visited her more and more frequently, yet mercifully the pain was not continuous, and during her times of relief from it she was almost back to her old optimistic and positive self, despite her feelings of physical weakness. By now Ada spent most of her time on the sofa in her London home and was pushed around by servants in her invalid chair when she wanted some fresh air. William was not often with her at this time.

Writing to her mother on Sunday January 10 1852, Ada notes:

It will be a long while before I shall have even average nervous energy. Everything is fatigue.

Yet in a burst of optimism, or perhaps to reassure Lady Byron, she adds:

But I am never in bad spirits, which is surprising.

On February 28 1852, her illness appears to be in remission but she adds:

There is still some *uncertainty* forever, & possibility of relapse. As I am certain I could not get thro any more severe illness, I shall not feel confident just yet…

It has been a very bad case… It is to me dreadful to know what the human frame *can* suffer, especially when I reflect there are even *worse* agonies than I have suffered.

Ada's life was made even more difficult by her having money worries due to the losses she had incurred in horse races. Finally, Lady Byron relented and told her lawyer that she would consider paying Ada's debts but that first Ada needed to supply a list of all the monies she owed.

In April 1852, Lady Byron's lawyer Stephen Lushington went to see Ada. He was a long-standing close friend of the family and had helped Lady Byron deftly through her separation from the defiant Byron, and had later married a close friend of hers. A formidable campaigner against slavery and capital punishment (1840), he was both a judge and Privy Counsellor. Lushington was shocked to see how ill Ada looked. She was weak, frail, much thinner than was healthy and was doing all she could do to cope with pain by taking laudanum and opium. Ada gave the discreet Lushington a list of the money she owed. (He was to spend the last two decades of his life on Lovelace's estate, dying in 1873.)

Lady Byron looked over the list carefully. She thought a hairdresser's bill ques-
tionable and also asked Lushington why Ada was spending money on opium. Lady
Byron herself indicated that she thought mesmerism would be better. Here, as often
during Ada's last year, it is puzzling that neither William nor Lady Byron spent much
time with Ada. Ada had servants to look after her, but Lady Byron especially, and
William too to some extent, seem to have felt that they didn't want to spend much
time with Ada when she was so ill. There is no clear evidence that explains why Lady
Byron and William behaved like this, though certainly Lady Byron felt that Ada's
illness was to some extent visited on her because of what Lady Byron saw as Ada's
misbehaviour in her life. In particular, Lady Byron, herself a hypochondriac, seems
to have both hated and feared illness. But Lady Byron may also have believed Ada's
illness to be a just punishment for the nature of the friendship Ada had had with
John Crosse.

Ada had got to know John Crosse through his brother Robert, a scientific
showman who enjoyed putting on elaborate demonstrations for the benefit of fee-
paying audience. She may have had an affair with Crosse. It appears that all the letters
John Crosse wrote to Ada were destroyed by Lady Byron after Ada's death, and that
Lady Byron paid John Crosse to return to her the letters Ada had written to him.
However, given her failing health and later death from ovarian cancer, sexual affairs
seem to be unlikely after the mid 1840s, around the time she met John Crosse.

The truth of the matter was that by the start of 1852 Ada was fatally ill, and that her
illness would subsequently turn into an agonising death. When writing to her mother,
however, she tried at first to downplay how ill she was, partly because she knew how
unsympathetic her mother could be towards illness suffered by anyone else.

However, as she got more and more ill, which she did in the early months of
1852, there seemed little point concealing from her mother just how unwell she really
was.

Babbage was friends with her all this time, as he had been since they had first met
in 1833, and he was deeply concerned about her health and her prognosis: indeed, he
was far more concerned than Lady Byron was.

In another letter to her mother which is undated, but was written on a Monday
evening some time early in 1852, Ada wrote the following terrible words about her
suffering:

When I find that not only one's whole being can become merely one living
agony, but that in that state, & *after* it, one's *mind* is gone more or less, – the
impression of *mortality* become appalling; & not of mortality merely, but of
mortality in an *agony* & *struggle*...

The more one suffers, the more appalling is it to feel that it may all be only in order to '*die like a dog*' as they say…

Mary Somerville was to observe: 'I never knew of anyone who suffered such protracted intolerable agony.' Sometime around the middle of August 1852, though the definite date is not known, Ada wrote to her mother in the familiar mixture of optimism and pessimism:

Tolerably comfortable now, & being let down *very easy*. I begin to understand *Death*, which is going on quietly & gradually every minute, & will never be a thing of one particular moment.

Ada tried to use what drugs she could to relieve her condition. She may even have taken cannabis. Her mother, on her part a keen follower of exotic new 'sciences' such as phrenology, suggested phrenomesmerism. Both Babbage and Faraday wrote sceptically about this and antagonised Lady Byron for life. Ada, however, knew her mother well and dutifully gave it a try. She wrote a letter to Lady Byron early in 1852, in effect answering her mother's query about the efficacy of mesmerism to deal with very severe pain:

I have heard a great deal about Cannabis from Sir G[eorge]. Wilkinson who is very familiar with it. It is not a thing to trifle with, but the effects… are *very definite*. I have got back to my old friend *Opium* and thankful enough. It seems mesmerism is powerless when I have my *real* pains, & not merely some slight cramps.

In happier times Ada, Lord Lovelace and their good friend Sir George Wilkinson had indulged Lady Byron in another one of her foibles – she was hardly alone in these, Augustus de Morgan was apparently taken by clairvoyance and spiritualism, as was his wife Sophia – and had visited a phrenologist called Deville. He claimed to be able to read the skull for personality traits. She was underwhelmed by the experience, especially when Deville felt Wilkinson's intellect rated higher than Lovelace's or hers.

The disease continued slowly to destroy Ada's body. On Friday May 7 1852, Ada wrote to her son Byron:

My dearest Son. I am quite a cripple & an *invalid*…

I am sadly distressed to think that during the few weeks *you* are likely to be with us, you will have a *sick Mama*, whom I fear a handsome active young fellow like you, will regard as a bore. Yet I think you are too good, & too aware of my *affection for you* & of my anxiety to see you again to be otherwise than my *affectionate son*, whether I am ill or well. *I* resign myself to my present state

& I trust will others.

Your most *affectionate Mother*

Lord Lovelace had originally condoned and even contributed financially to Ada's betting, and perhaps even encouraged it, but when he could no longer deal with the money side, he threw himself on Lady Byron's mercy in the hope she would help out. His attempt was charmless, but he could not have made a more serious mistake. Lady Byron had intended William to be Ada's protector in the way that Byron had singularly failed to be. Instead of providing a comfortable moat behind which her fragile daughter would be safe, he himself now came to her with the appalling evidence she needed to see that he had aided and abetted in her ruin.

She quickly regained her daughter's trust by helping Ada pay off a pawn shop that had a diamond from her husband's family. Soon the control Lady Byron had had over her daughter in her youth was re-established. As Ada's illness got worse and worse, Lady Byron moved into Ada and William's house at 6 Cumberland Place, on August 22 1852, ostensibly to look after her but in fact to boss her (and him) about.

She dismissed Ada and William's servants at Great Cumberland Place, replacing them with servants of her own. Lady Byron discouraged William from visiting Ada too often, even though it was his own house. However, by all accounts William stood up to his formidable mother-in-law in this respect, though he did leave a note saying that in his absence Lady Byron would be master of the house.

Babbage is known to have visited Ada one last time at Great Cumberland Place on Thursday August 12 1852. After this visit, Lady Byron did not allow Babbage to visit her any more. Lady Byron and Babbage appear to have had a row that day. Ada wanted Babbage to be the executor of her will and gave him a letter to give him legal authority to do this. Fatefully he agreed to do so for his dying friend, earning Lady Byron's eternal wrath. He had agreed to insert himself between her and her daughter without being consulted, something she resented violently. Like all Ada's attempts to escape her mother's influence, this one was doomed, too. The letter turned out to lack sufficient legal authority to empower Babbage.

On August 12 Lady Byron also told Ada that John Crosse would no longer be allowed to visit her. He and Ada were clearly still close friends. But Ada took her own subtle, last revenge on her mother, and stipulated that she was to be buried next to her father. William wrote; 'She walked about the room on my arm for a time, speaking almost with satisfaction of the posthumous arrangements & simple inscription to the effect that she was placed by his side by her own desire.' She also stipulated during this time endowments to various people, including the nurses, although it wasn't clear where the money might come from.

August 12 was the last day Babbage saw Ada. Also, after that day, letters Ada ostensibly wrote cannot definitely be attributed to her, as Lady Byron very likely had part in their composition as she had in her youth. Babbage himself stated that Ada had no control of her house or life from that day forward.

One man who was allowed to visit, however, was Charles Dickens. It is difficult to know how well Ada knew Charles Dickens's work, but she was at least evidently familiar with his novel *Dombey and Son*, which had been published recently, in 1848. Dickens, born February 7 1812, was a few months short of being four years older than Ada. On Thursday August 19 1852, a week after Babbage saw Ada for the last time, Charles Dickens went to visit her and to read to her.

Ada and Dickens were friends from when she first entered London society, though it is impossible to trace the friendship because Ada's letters to Dickens have not survived. Ada did, however, write to her husband (most likely in 1842, but the letter is undated) to express her delight in Dickens's *American Notes*, which were published in October 1842. As she wrote to William:

> I am as happy as possible & in great spirits. I have read a quantity of Dickens's *American Notes*, which would delight even you.
>
> There is so much elegance and refinement in all his jokes; such real wit, such original ideas & comparisons, & such profound remarks, & always kindly and high moral tone, that he cannot but captivate the impartial I think in this work.

Dickens had been part of Ada and Babbage's circle since the late 1830s. Five of his letters to her are contained in Dickens's collected letters. They suggest a good friendship but not an emotionally intimate one. It is clear, though, that Dickens sometimes called on Ada in London. Ada, Babbage and William sometimes attended dinner parties at Dickens's home at Devonshire Place. Babbage may perhaps have accompanied Ada if William wasn't available. They lived within a mile from each other and William was often at one of his country houses, Ockham or Ashley to deal with his tunnels.

Ada most likely got to know Dickens through Babbage. From the years 1839 to 1851, Babbage and Dickens lived only a few hundred yards from each other; Dickens in his large house on Devonshire Terrace in Marylebone Road, and Babbage in Dorset Street.

Dickens was most certainly not of a scientific disposition or frame of mind, and had little or no technical knowledge of Babbage's work. But he had no problem understanding the benefit to mankind and freedom from mental drudgery that a calculation machine would bring. Writing from Broadstairs, Kent, to his brother Henry Austin on December 20 1851 about the soaring costs of the modifications to his new house in London's Tavistock Place, Dickens was ruefully and ironically to comment that the bill submitted by the builder was 'too long to be added up, until Babbage's Calculating Machine shall be improved and finished... there is not paper enough ready-made, to carry it over and bring it forward again.'

A crucial theme in Dickens's novel *Little Dorrit* (1857) is how the cold and indifferent workings of the law and government bring human misery. The tenth chapter of the first part of the book, entitled with transparent irony 'Containing the Whole Science of Government', focuses on a Government department dedicated to never getting anything done. Dickens calls it the 'Circumlocution Office'.

> The Circumlocution Office was (as everybody knows without being told) the most important Department under government. No public business of any kind could possibly be done without the acquiescence of the Circumlocution Office... Whatever was required to be done, the Circumlocution Office was beforehand with all the public departments in the art of perceiving – HOW NOT TO DO IT.... Through this delicate perception, through the tact with which it invariably seized it, and through the genius with which it always acted on it, the Circumlocution Office had risen to overtop all the public departments; and the public condition had risen to be – what it was.

One of the most put-upon victims of the Circumlocution Office is an inventor called Daniel Doyce. Dickens describes him as a 'a quiet, plain, steady man', who 'seemed a little depressed, but neither ashamed nor repentant.'

We are told that a dozen years earlier, Doyce has perfected 'an invention (involving a very curious secret process) of great importance to his country and his fellow creatures'. But instead of winning praise from officialdom for what he has done, from the moment Doyce approaches the Government for help with funding, he 'ceases to be an innocent citizen, and becomes a culprit. He is treated, from that instant, as a man who has done some infernal action.'

Dickens's imagination got by perfectly well, most of the time, without needing to use real people as the basis for all the characters he created. The similarities between Doyce and Babbage, though, are too striking to be ignored. The description of Doyce's appearance is a good fit to Babbage to begin with ('... a practical looking man, whose hair had turned grey, and in whose face and forehead there were deep lines of cogitation') and even the timing of when Doyce 'perfected' his invention ('a dozen years ago') which after all is an entirely free choice on Dickens's part, seems to have been chosen very deliberately to allude to Babbage's work. As for the account of the invention itself, its 'great importance to his country and his fellow creatures' also seems to point directly at Babbage, as does the ironic account of Doyce's plight voiced by another character, Mr Meagles:

> '... [H]e has been ingenious, and he has been trying to turn his ingenuity to his country's service. That makes him a public offender, sir.'

And what Doyce says about how inventors such as he are treated at home compared with abroad could easily have been words taken down pretty well verbatim from some lament Babbage might, in a self-pitying mood, have made at one of Dickens's numerous dinner parties at Devonshire Terrace, over the turtle soup, the turbot or the roast lamb.

'Yes. No doubt I am disappointed. Hurt? Yes. No doubt I am hurt. That's only natural. But what I mean, when I say that people who put themselves in the same position, are mostly used in the same way – '

'In England,' said Mr Meagles.

'Oh! of course I mean in England. When they take their inventions into foreign countries, that's quite different. And that's the reason why so many go there.'

On the day when Dickens visited Ada to read to her, there is no record of Lady Byron being present. However, William was on this occasion. Ada had asked Dickens to come to read to her the death scene from *Dombey and Son*, in which little Paul Dombey dies. As William wrote, Ada 'expressed a strong wish to see Ch. Dickens – the passage about the death of the boy in his Dombey on the shores of the ocean had struck her & she wished him to know her sympathy and I wrote to him to hasten if he would see her alive.'

The passage where little Paul Dombey dies, was, by 1852, already one of the most famous in Victorian literature. The novel is about how the cold, unfeeling, haughty businessman Mr Dombey – the embodiment of nineteenth-century man, steely arrogance and pride – is slowly softened by the reviving, refreshing fountain of feminine life represented by his daughter Florence, who grows to be a woman and is older than her brother Paul. In this scene, she is 'Floy'. In many ways, the novel echoes many aspects of Ada's life: masculinity stubbornly repressing the female spirit and refusing to see anything in women except ornamental charm and intellectual inferiority.

Little Paul is about five years old when he dies:

Sister and brother wound their arms around each other, and the golden light came streaming in, and fell upon them, locked together.

'How fast the river runs, between its green banks and the rushes, 'Floy! But it's very near the sea. I hear the waves! They always said so!'

Presently he told her the motion of the boat upon the stream was lulling him to rest. How green the banks were now, how bright the flowers growing on them, and how tall the rushes! Now the boat was out at sea, but gliding smoothly on. And now there was a shore before him. Who stood on the bank – !

He put his hands together, as he had been used to do at his prayers. He did not remove his arms to do it; but they saw him fold them so, behind her neck.

'Mama is like you, Floy. I know her by the face! But tell them that the print upon the stairs at school is not divine enough. The light about the head is shining on me as I go!'

The golden ripple on the wall came back again, and nothing else stirred in the room. The old, old fashion! The fashion that came in with our first garments, and will last unchanged until our race has run its course, and the wide firmament is rolled up like a scroll. The old, old fashion – Death!

Oh thank GOD, all who see it, for that older fashion yet, of Immortality! And look upon us, angels of young children, with regards not quite estranged, when the swift river bears us to the ocean!

Ada and Dickens evidently discussed life more generally at this meeting. William wrote that Ada spoke to him afterwards of 'the comfort she had derived from the concurrence of their ideas about the future.' As George Orwell pointed out in his long essay on Dickens, Dickens seems almost unaware of the future and it seems more likely that 'future' is William's euphemistic term for what they really discussed – her death.

Ada at that moment had only a few months to live. The appalling diagnosis, which one of her doctors, Dr West, gave, has survived:

Lady Lovelace's disease is cancer; the final symptoms of which appeared between eighteen months and two years ago; consisting not in pain but in frequent and alarmingly profuse haemorrhages. In December the haemor-rhages ceased but pain began to be experienced, which has increased in frequency and intensity up to the present time; and coupled with which there has been an advance of the disease: an extension of it to other organs. A condition such as hers is thus a very grievous one; there is not merely a local disorder increasing daily in a situation in which surgical dexterity can effect nothing, but the blood itself is poisoned, and our remedies cannot reach to that. The duty of the physician is thus a very sad one; as the highest success which he can hope to attain is to secure not recovery, but euthanasia.

The medical science of Ada's day could do nothing to cure her, and unfortu-nately nothing much to alleviate her suffering either.

The hypodermic needle had not yet been invented, and the only way to administer opiates was orally, which made them much less effective than if they were directly introduced into the bloodstream.

On Wednesday August 25 1852, just six days after visiting Ada and reading to her, Dickens wrote a letter to his friend the philanthropist Angela Burdett-Coutts about the visit.

> The night before I left town (last Saturday) I had a note from Lord Lovelace to tell me that Lady Lovelace was dying, and that the death of the child in *Dombey* had been so much in her thoughts and had soothed her so, that she wished to see me once more if I could be found. I went, and sat alone with her for some time. It was very solemn and sad, but her fortitude was quite surprising; and her Conviction that all the agony she has suffered (which has been very great) had some good design in the goodness of God, impressed me very much.

By 'last Saturday' Dickens may be referring to Saturday August 14 rather than the Saturday (August 21) preceding his writing of this letter. There is a slight implication in what Dickens says that he went to read to Ada on the same day when Lord Lovelace told him how ill Ada was, but in fact he did not read to her until five days later, on Thursday. The fact that Dickens evidently did not know Ada was dying suggests that perhaps they had not seen much of each other for a while.

William, Lord Lovelace, 1850.

On August 30 her pulse stopped for ten minutes, but still she did not die. Her agony increased, and she was incoherent where she had previously been resigned, and feared she would be buried alive. Previously an agnostic, she now begged her religious mother and William to pray for her. Lady Byron wrote it was 'the best moment she has had', it appears that she meant 'that her father had sent her this disease, & doomed her to an early death! She spoke of it as cruel, & unjust of God to allow it.'

On September 1, at Lady Byron's prompting, Ada confessed her sins (whatever they were) to William. He walked out of the room devastated and remained silent about what was revealed to him until his death. William's handwriting was normally like a pigeon's scrawl, and yet, in very clear handwriting he wrote that if he was absent it should be known that 'Lady Byron is the mistress of my house'. And Ada was no longer, 'Our Bird.'

Ada still had much pain to suffer before she died on November 27 1852, after suffering appalling pain that was only partly relieved by the laudanum and by a new drug, chloroform.

Lady Byron and Ada's husband William were at her bedside when she died – he was allowed in at this stage.

A week after her death, Ada was laid to rest next to her father in the small church in the village of Hucknall Torkard, Nottinghamshire, close to Lord Byron's ancestral home of Newstead Abbey. The father and daughter – whose lives were almost exactly the same length, now lie side by side in a tomb that has been permanently sealed since 1929.

A detailed report of Ada's funeral appeared in the *Nottinghamshire Guardian* on Wednesday December 8 1852. The report reads as follows:

FUNERAL OF THE COUNTESS OF LOVELACE

On Friday last the remains of the Hon. Augusta Ada, Countess of Lovelace, the ... remains of the deceased countess were conveyed privately from Great Cumberland Place, London, where she expired, to the George the Fourth Hotel, Nottingham. The body lay in state during Thursday night, and was visited by a large number of the inhabitants of the town.

The ceremony had a very pleasing and solemn effect. The room was draped with black cloth, and the floor, where the body lay, was covered with the same. The coffin was placed in the centre, bearing a silk velvet cushion with her ladyship's coronet resting at the foot, and the Lovelace arms richly emblazoned at the head.

Twelve wax tapers were kept burning, six on either side of the coffin. On the following morning the body was conveyed by the old road to Hucknall Torkard. The mourners consisting of the Earl of Lovelace, Lord Byron, the Hon. Locke King, Sir G. Crauford, Mr King, Dr Lushington [Lady Byron's lawyer], Col. Wildman, Woronzow Greig, Esq. [Ada's lawyer], and Mr C. Noel were brought by special train to Hucknall. The funeral *cortege* was formed in the station yard in the following order:

Two mutes on horseback.

Her Ladyship's Coronet, upon a crimson velvet cushion, covered with black crape, borne by an attendant upon a richly caparisoned and plumed horse.

THE HEARSE, drawn by four horses, profusely caparisoned with feathers, velvet equipments and velvet hammer-cloths, on which were large coronets, decorated also with plumes of ostrich feathers, and emblazoned with the hatchments of the deceased.

MOURNING COACH, drawn by four horses, containing the Earl of Lovelace, Lord Byron, the Honourable Locke King, and Sir G. Crauford.

MOURNING COACH, drawn by four horses, containing – King, Esq., Dr Lushington, and Woronsow [sic] Greig, Esq.

MOURNING COACH, drawn by four horses, containing Colonel Wildman, Mr C. Noel, and Sir George Wilkinson.

The private carriage of Colonel Wildman, of Newstead Abbey.

The procession then moved forward at a funeral pace through the village to the parish church, at the entrance to which it was received by the Rev. Curtis Jackson, perpetual curate, who, reading the funeral service, preceded the procession into the church, where the body was placed in the centre aisle.

The coffin was covered with rich puce coloured silk velvet, with silver furniture, bearing a massive raised shield, upon which were chased the emblazonments and family arms, surmounted with the Countess's coronet, in silver. The plate bore the following inscription:

The Right Honourable Augusta Ada, wife of
WILLIAM, EARL OF LOVELACE, and only daughter of GEORGE GORDON NOEL, LORD BYRON
Born December 10th, 1815,
Died November 27th, 1852.
Aged 37 years. [This is an error: when she died Ada was only 36, like her father; the family must have thought she would survive another two weeks to reach her 37th birthday when they commissioned her tombstone.]

The service was proceeded with amidst the deepest silence and the most reverential attention of the numerous spectators, many of whom were much affected. The body was then placed in the vault adjoining the remains of the father. In the vault there are now seventeen coffins. The first that attracts the eye is the coffin of the late poet-lord, placed on that of his mother, at the head of which stands the urn which contains his heart and brains, as brought from Greece. On the top of the coffin is his coronet, very much decayed and reduced.

The coffin is in a very good state of preservation. Close to it is now laid the body of the late Countess, having the coronet placed in the centre of the coffin. Many of the coffins are now very much decayed, nothing being left but the leaden shells, some of which very plainly show their antiquity.

After giving some biographical information about Ada, the report goes on to give a description of the location of the village and of the words on the tablet to Byron's memory. The report concludes:

After the funeral the numerous spectators of the ceremony were gratified with an inspection of the vault. Some of them, as we heard them afterwards boasting, succeeded in bearing away precious relics from the poet's shrine, in the shape of small fragments of scarlet cloth, torn from his mouldering coffin.

Lady Byron did not attend the funeral of her daughter, perhaps preferring a cure to reports that she had forgiven her deceased husband. Nor did Babbage attend the funeral. Probably he felt that as he and Lady Byron had fallen out, it would not have been appropriate for him to attend. If he had heard rumours that Lady Byron might not attend, he doubtless did not want to meet her and cause a scene in case the rumours were untrue. Besides, the Ada he had known and maybe loved was gone now.

$\mathscr{R}$edemption

Lady Byron would live on until her death of breast cancer on May 16 1860, at the age of 67. She had told the story of Byron's incestuous relationship to Harriet Beecher Stowe, who published this account nine years later. The posthumous information she had given Beecher Stowe demolished Lord Byron's acclaim as a romantic figure for Britain at large.

While it is tempting to cast Lady Byron's role in Ada Lovelace's life as a maternal equivalent of P.G. Woodehouse's Aunt Agatha, in matters other than her daughter she was mellower. She remained steadfast in her support of the abolition of slavery and attended the second World Conference against Slavery in London, 1843 as a very small band of women despite having expressly been excluded from attending. She also appears to have been loved by her spa friends. Sophia de Morgan, the daughter of her tutor and wife of Augustus de Morgan wrote warmly:

> Lady Byron was always shy with strangers, especially with those who excited her veneration. This shyness gave her an appearance of coldness, but she and my husband soon knew each other's worth, and she never lost an opportunity of showing her regard for him and trust in his judgment. He was rather surprised to find in one commonly reputed to be hard and austere, qualities of quite an opposite nature. She was impulsive and affectionate almost to a fault, but the expression of her feelings was often checked by the habitual state of repression in which the circumstances of her life had placed her.

And Babbage?

He continued to labour on his dream of cogwheel computers for almost another twenty years, but his heart had gone out of the enterprise, and it never bore any fruit. He was, indeed, still working on his designs for the Analytical Engine when, after a short illness, he died on October 18 1871, aged nearly eighty.

Lady Byron had died on May 16 1860. William, who married again in 1865 and had another child, a son, by his second wife Jane Jenkins, lived until December 29 1893.

In Babbage's last years he was plagued by headaches and the noise of urban life. He socialised little, spending much time alone in his London home, living among the ghosts of his dreams.

A precious but tragic insight into Babbage's forlorn later life was provided at a mathematical conference in July 1914 by Lord Moulton, a man born in 1844 who enjoyed all the privileges of his class and became a prize-winning mathematician, barrister, judge and statesman. Recalling a visit he had made to Babbage many years earlier, apparently in the late 1860s, Moulton painted a dismal picture of the price the gods had extracted from Babbage for having bestowed on him a vision of a computer, without granting him the tools – technological, financial, and diplomatic – to make his dreams come true.

One of the sad memories of my life is a visit to the celebrated mathematician and inventor, Mr Babbage. He was far advanced in age, but his mind was still as vigorous as ever. He took me through his work rooms. In the first room I saw the parts of the original Calculating Machine, which had been shown in an incomplete state many years before. I asked him about its present form.

'I have not finished it because in working at it I came on the idea of my Analytical Machine, which would do all that it was capable of doing and much more. Indeed, the idea was so much simpler that it would have taken more work to complete the Calculating Machine than to design and construct the other in its entirety, so I turned my attention to the Analytical Machine.'

After a few minutes' talk we went into the next work-room, where he showed and explained to me the working of the elements of the Analytical Machine. I asked if I could see it.

'I have never completed it,' he said, 'because I hit upon an idea of doing the same thing by a different and far more effective method, and this rendered it useless to proceed on the old lines.' Then we went into the third room. There lay scattered bits of mechanism but I saw no trace of any working machine.

Very cautiously I approached the subject, and received the dreaded answer, 'It is not constructed yet, but I am working at it, and it will take less time to construct it altogether than it would have taken to complete the Analytical Machine from the stage in which I left it.'

I took leave of the old man with a heavy heart. When he died a few years later, not only had he constructed no machine, but the verdict of a jury of kind and sympathetic scientific men who were deputed to pronounce upon what he had left behind him, either in papers or mechanism, was that everything was too incomplete to be capable of being put to any useful purpose.

The 'kind and sympathetic scientific men' were wrong and their decision may be described as one of the greatest blunders in the history of science – with the benefit of hindsight. It would take a hundred years for scientists to understand what Ada had grasped when scientists finally resumed the leap forward that could have been made in the 1840s. Ironically, Ada's *Notes* would play a key role in the rehabilitation of Babbage's reputation.

The (cultural) myopia of the kind men was mirrored by the somewhat condescending tone in which Ada's tutor Augustus de Morgan had judged her *Notes* on Babbage's machine. Lady Byron had sent some of Ada's early drafts to him in 1841:

> The tract about Babbage's machine is a pretty thing enough, but I could I think produce a series of extracts, out of Lady Lovelace's first queries upon new subjects, which would make a mathematician see that it was no criterion of what might be expected from her.

As things turned out, Babbage had left behind enough plans and drawings for a complete, working version of one of his machines to be constructed by an epoch that was better equipped to understand his vision. All he had really needed was access to an effective and efficient precision engineering industry: not because the technology of his own time was not up to the job of producing components to the requisite tolerances – it was – but because Babbage required a reliable source of thousands of identical cogwheels to be supplied relatively promptly, and at a reasonable cost.

If Babbage had let Ada manage his affairs, as she so much wished to do, everything he had hoped to achieve might have been achieved. She would have been better suited to direct his engineers and even his financial affairs with greater charm, clarity and effectiveness, getting the best value for money from those who helped him make his cogwheels and his other spare parts.

As for Ada's vision of a machine that could process and memorise calculations, algebraic patterns and even all types of symbolic relationships as adeptly as the Jacquard loom could weave silk, that was a dream just waiting to come true.

She had seen the computer age clearly ahead. She just was never allowed to act on what she saw.

The dream began to start coming true in 1881, when a young engineer, William J. Hammer, who was working in Thomas Edison's laboratory in Menlo Park, New Jersey, made an accidental discovery that turned out to be of great importance. He discovered an inexplicable current in an evacuated vacuum tube that turned out to lead to the discovery of electrons.

The modern computer evolved from an electromagnetic device, the Harvard Mark 1, sponsored by IBM, which was built and first operated in 1944. It is arguable that there is a link between the Jacquard loom and this machine, because IBM, formerly International Business Machines, was a direct descendant of a company founded by a German-born inventor, Herman Hollerith, which pioneered the use of 'tabulators' that processed punched cards. The idea for these tabulators was probably inspired by the Jacquard loom.

One of the strangest things about Babbage's work is that there is no direct line of descent between the Difference Engine and the Analytical Engine and the modern computer. When Howard Aiken, the brains behind the Harvard Mark 1, announced its completion to an astonished world at a press conference in 1944, he paid a fulsome tribute to Babbage and famously said:

If Babbage had lived seventy-five years later, I would have been out of a job.

However, at that point in the history of science, Babbage was a close to forgotten figure, only remembered by a few computer pioneers.

Alan Turing, the British mathematician and code-breaker who in the 1940s and 1950s laid many of the intellectual foundations necessary for the invention of the modern computer, was aware of Ada's writings.

Turing discussed the assertion that computers are incapable of originality. He called this the 'Lovelace objection', because, according to Ada, machines are incapable of independent learning. We have already seen that Ada wrote the following:

The Analytical Engine has no pretensions whatever to *originate* anything. It can do whatever we *know how to order it* to perform. It can *follow* analysis; but it has no power of *anticipating* any analytical relations or truths. Its province is to assist us in making *available* what we are already acquainted with.

Turing suggested that Ada's comment can be reduced to the assertion that computers 'can never take us by surprise'. Turing said, however, that on the contrary, computers could still surprise humans, in particular where the consequences of different facts are not immediately recognizable. Turing also suggested that Ada was hampered by the context from which she wrote, and that in truth the way the brain stores and processes information would be quite similar to that of a computer.

Babbage's work came under fresh scrutiny in the 1970s, partly as a result of the devoted research of the late Dr Allan Bromley. Any book that looks at Babbage's work and what the modern world has made of it owes a debt to Dr Bromley.

The successful building, in 1991, of a full-size working version of the Difference Engine – the version Babbage himself called Difference Engine number 2 – is unquestionably one of the most wonderful stories in the history of science. *The Cogwheel Brain*, by Doron Swade, who master-minded and led the project to build the machine – and nine years later, a no less thrilling project to build the printer – is a unique source of information about Babbage's life and the modern realisation of Babbage's dreams.

Babbage's increased fame has led to Ada's fame increasing too. Ada's fame is, as we've seen, of a different order. It is no exaggeration to say that she understood where Babbage's work would lead better than he ever did.

Afterword

While Bifrons, in Patrixbourne near Canterbury, has now been demolished, the little bridge is still here. It is readily visible from the road between Patrixbourne and Bridge, and is less than a hundred yards from the road.

It was there, too, at the time Ada spent her often lonely year at Bifrons in 1828. I am sure she often wandered down to the bridge from the house, and perhaps she glanced with some envy at village children playing in the adjacent field beyond the road, and wondered why she couldn't have more friends. I think she must have stood on the bridge and watched the Nailbourne flow under her. She might have glanced above her and seen birds flying and thought, yet again, how one day she planned to find a way of flying herself.

Today, if you stand on that bridge and look skywards, you will see the occasional jet airliner pass by on the flight path towards Eastern Europe or back from there towards London. Ada never saw those planes flying, but her spirit did.

We may, too, think of the following, from the final lines of the third canto of *Childe Harolde*, in which Byron addresses his daughter.

Yet, though dull Hate as duty should be taught,
I know that that thou wilt love me; though my name,
Should be shut from thee, as a spell still fraught
With desolation, – and a broken claim:
Though the grave closed between us, – 'twere the same,
I know that thou wilt love me; though to drain
My blood from out thy being were an aim,
And an attainment, – all would be in vain, -
Still thou would'st love me, still that more than life retain.

$\mathcal{N}$otes

1 May Gray. Gray was Scottish, and fond of discipline. Her sister Agnes had previously been Byron's nursemaid. I haven't been able to find out exactly how old May was when she looked after Byron, but judging from the fact that by 1798, a married Agnes was living in Woodside, a working-class district of Aberdeen, with two children of her own, it seems logical to assume that May was younger than Agnes and that Agnes was in her late teens or early twenties by 1798. This would mean that May was probably about seventeen or eighteen when she was Byron's nursemaid.

2 From Trinity College (Cambridge) Archivist Jon Smith.

3 The date of Babbage's wife Georgiana's death was discovered by Annelisa Christensen who assisted me with the research for this book. The date is mentioned in an issue of the London *Times* for September 1827, which records the death as having happened 'on the 1st inst at Boughton-house, in the county of Worcester, aged 35, Georgiana, the wife of Charles Babbage Esq., of Devonshire-street, Portland-place.'

4 The exact date of his daughter Georgiana's death isn't found in Anthony Hyman's standard biography of Babbage; Hyman just gives the year 1834. But Anne Christensen, researching the details of Babbage's daughter Georgiana's death for this book, found a reference to Georgiana's death in the London newspaper *The Standard* for September 30 1834. (Admittedly Hyman did not have the advantage of access to on-line newspaper archives.)

Sources

I wish especially to acknowledge one particular source, *Ada, The Enchantress of Numbers* by Betty Alexandra Toole. Her book contains all Ada's letters to Babbage, as well as many other letters between Ada and a wide range of people, including Lady Byron. The book also contains Babbage's letter from Ada to Babbage in which he mentions the phrase 'Enchantress of Number'. The site of Bifrons house is close by Patrixbourne village, and is accessible via a path close by the mini-roundabout just outside Patrixbourne. In order in which they appear in the book, the following sources were used:

Lovelace-Byron Papers, Bodleian Library, Oxford, with kind permission of Lord Lytton

The Memoirs of John Addington Symonds

The Woeful Victorian by Phyllis Grosskurth (Holt, Rinehart and Winston, New York, 1964)

Annabella's letter to Byron on Sunday, August 22, 1813, which rekindled their relationship is in the Lovelace-Byron Papers. It is almost completely legible.

Benjamin Disraeli *Venetia* (1837)

Toole, JJ O'Connor and E.F. Robertson's article on Mary Somerville. http://www-history.mcs.st-andrews.ac.uk/Biographies/Somer-ville.html

Woronzow Greig's short and often illegible biography of Ada is in the Lovelace-Byron Papers.

Jacquard's Web by James Essinger My main source for the early history of Jacquard's life are papers published in the *Bulletin Municipal Officiel* of Lyons between 1998 and 1999.

A History of Textiles by Kax Wilson (Westview Press, Boulder, Colorado, 1979)

The Fontana History of Technology by Donald Cardwell (Fontana Press, London, 1994)

On the subject of Babbage's personal life, there is an intriguing letter to him from a Reverend Lunn in Add. MSS 37,185, folio 310. This suggests that Babbage had asked Lunn to enquire about a potentially suitable candidate for a wife for Babbage

Charles Babbage's *Passage from the Life of a Philosopher*, and his archive, held by the British Library.

Herschel to Babbage urging the abandonment of formality in correspondence is in Volume 2 of the Herschel Papers in the library of the Royal Society, London. Folio 8.

The draft letter from Charles Babbage to Jean Arago is in the British Library, Additional Manuscripts No. 37,191 folios 287-9.

The portrait of Jacquard which Babbage was finally able to obtain is on display in the Babbage exhibition in the Science Museum, London.

Jean Arago's letter explaining his problems with obtaining the Jacquard portrait for Babbage is in the British Library, Additional Manuscripts No. 37,191, folio 316.

The evidence for when Babbage returned to Britain from Turin is inherent in a letter in Add. MSS 39,191, folio 450. This is dated 11 September 1840. It was addressed to Babbage in London but redirected to an address in Ostend, where he seems to have been staying prior to coming back to Britain.

Sketch of the Analytical Engine, invented by Charles Babbage, Esq. [by L.F. Menabrea, with notes by Ada Lovelace] *Scientific Memoirs, iii, p 666-731 www.fourmilab.ch/babbage/sketch.html*

Sir Robert Peel's letter to the Earl of Haddington about the correct attitude to adopt to the financial requests of men of science is in the British Library's Additional Manuscripts 40,456, folio 98.

Peel's letter to Buckland, showing how the Prime Minister felt about Babbage, is in Add. MSS 40,514 folio 223.

Henry Goulburn's letter to Babbage notifying him of the Government's decision to stop funding the Difference Engine, is in Add. MSS V 37,192 f 172-173

Babbage's detailed account of his abortive meeting with Sir Robert Peel on Friday, 11 November 1842 is in Add. MSS 37,192, folio 189.

Although I do not mention this directly in the text, for details of a dinner-party given by Dickens which Babbage, Lord and Lady Lovelace attended see *The Letters of Charles Dickens Vol. 5 1847-1849*, p. 513 ed. Storey/Fielding (OUP, Oxford, 1981).

For Dickens's letter to his brother-in-law, the architect and artist Henry Austin, about the bill for Tavistock Place, see *The Letters of Charles Dickens Vol. 6*, p. 556 ed. Storey/Tillotson and Burgis (OUP, Oxford, 1988).

The diagnosis by Dr West is in the Lovelace-Byron Papers.

The account of Ada's funeral appeared in the *Nottinghamshire Guardian* on Wednesday December 8 1852. It was found by Annelisa Christensen.

A Manual of Operation for the Automatic Sequence Controlled Calculator by Howard Aiken (Harvard University Press, Cambridge, Massachusetts, 1946 and Herman Hollerith, *Forgotten Giant of Information Processing* by Geoffrey D. Austrian (Columbia University Press, New York, 1982

Further Reading

Aspray, William (Editor), *Computing Before Computers*. Ames, Iowa: Iowa State University Press, 1990.

Babbage, Charles. *On the Economy of Machinery and Manufactures*. London: Charles Knight, 1832.

Babbage, Charles. *On the Principles and Development of the Calculator*. New York: Dover Publications, Inc., 1961.

Babbage, Charles. *Passages from the Life of a Philosopher*. New Brunswick, New Jersey: Rutgers University Press and Piscataway, New Jersey: IEEE Press, 1994.

Babbage, Charles. *Science and Reform, Selected Works of Charles Babbage*. Cambridge: Cambridge University Press, 1989.

Bromley, Allan. *The Babbage Papers in the Science Museum*. London: The Science Museum, 1991.

Brown, Donald. *Charles Babbage – The Man and his Machine*. Totnes: The Totnes Museum Study Centre, 1992.

Byron, Lord. *The Works of Lord Byron*. Wordsworth Editions. 1994.

Buxton, H.W. *Memoir of the Life and Labours of the Late Charles Babbage Esq. F.R.S.*. Cambridge, Massachusetts: The MIT Press and Tomash Publishers (Los Angeles / San Francisco), 1988.

Campbell-Kelly, Martin and William Aspray. *Computer: A History of the Information Machine*. New York: HarperCollins, 1986.

Collier, Bruce. *The Little Engines that Could've*. New York & London Garland Publishing: 1990.

Dickens, Charles. *The Letters of Charles Dickens: 1820 – 1870* (2nd release). Electronic edition.

Dickens, Charles. *Little Dorrit*. London: Chapman & Hall, 1855.

Eisler, Benita. *Byron*. London: Hamish Hamilton, 1999.

Essinger, James. *Jacquard's Web*. Oxford: Oxford University Press. 2004.

Grosskurth, Phyllis. *Byron, The Flawed Angel*. London: Hodder and Stoughton, 1997.

Hyman, Anthony. *Charles Babbage, Pioneer of the Computer*. Oxford: Oxford University Press, 1982.

King-Hele, D. G. (Editor), *John Herschel 1792-1871: A Bicentennial Commemoration*. London: The Royal Society, 1992.

Knowles, James Sheridan. *Love, a play in five acts*. [First US edition]. Baltimore, H.A. Turner. c 1840.

Lethbridge, Lucy. *Ada Lovelace, computer wizard of Victorian England*. London: Short Books 2004.

Maddox, Brenda. *Rosalind Franklin, the dark lady of DNA*. London. Harper Collins 2002.

Moore, Doris Langley. *Ada: Countess of Lovelace: Byron's Legitimate Daughter*. London: John Murray, 1977.

Moseley, Maboth. *Irascible Genius: A Life of Charles Babbage, Inventor*. London: Hutchinson, 1964.

Snyder, Laura J. *The Philosophical Breakfast Club*. New York: Random House, 2011.

Stein, Dorothy. *Ada: A Life and Legacy*. Cambridge, Massachusetts: MIT Press, 1985.

Swade, Doron. *Charles Babbage and his Calculating Engines*. London: The Science Museum, 1991.

Swade, Doron. *The Cogwheel Brain*. London: Little, Brown and Company (UK), 2000.

Toole, Betty. *Ada, the Enchantress of Numbers*. Mill Valley, California: Strawberry Press, 1992.

Woolley, Benjamin. *The Bride of Science*. London: Macmillan, 1999.

$\mathscr{A}$cknowledgements

My sincere thanks to my publisher and discerning, insightful and hard-working editor Martin Rynja of Gibson Square, and my agent Diane Banks. Diane is an agent and ally of the very highest calibre.

My great thanks to Ada's descendant the Earl of Lytton for granting me access to the Lovelace-Byron Collection in the Bodleian Library, Oxford, and for permission to reproduce material from it. My thanks also to the Earl of Lytton's literary executors, Laurence Pollinger Limited.

Alexandra Toole's superb book *Ada, the Enchantress of Numbers* (1992) has been an essential companion to me during the writing of *A Female Genius*, as have been my conversations with my friend Alexandra herself.

My very sincere thanks to Laurence Green, Alexander Dembitz and Briony Kapoor for their support and friendship. My deep gratitude also to Helen Komatsu (formerly Helen Wylie), with whom I have had so many conversations about Ada and Babbage; to Russell Galen in New York for kindly editing the early sample material of this book; to Annelisa Lynch for her wonderfully ingenious and dedicated research and advice; and to Fiona Godfrey for being my amanuensis for this project and for her excellent editing and our many helpful discussions about Ada and Ada's world.

Many thanks also to Dr Doron Swade MBE for his friendship and for his generosity with his time over several years, and to Ada enthusiast and expert Dr Betty Alexandra Toole for her help.

I would additionally like to express my gratitude to: Margaret Dowley MBE; Jackie Hammond; Andrew Greet IM; Nicole Roberts, Stephen Gillatt, Maurice Raraty; Meriel Connor; John Sullivan; Jonathan Smith and Sandy Paul of Trinity College, Cambridge; Joanna Corden and Keith Moore of the Royal Society in London; Colin Harris and his team at the Bodleian Library, Oxford and also to Mary Clapinson there; J.J. O'Connor and E.F. Robertson for their excellent work on Mary Somerville, from which I have drawn; the late Bruce Collier; Professor Anthony Hyman; Tony Redding; Philippa Redding; Ranjit Bolt OBE; Richard Gill, Mike Kinder and Neil Roberts, who all taught me at Wyggeston Boys' Grammar School in Leicester; Evzen Kolar, the Hollywood producer of the movie *Enchantress of Numbers*; my computer consultant Mike Anderson; my brilliant and ever-helpful domestic colleague Kimmy Taylor; my tolerant and patient former bank manager Mike Hatton; Clair-Marie Slater; Bruce Todd; Sally Day; Sandy Baker; Barbara Lammers; Jennifer O'Leary; Heather Rowland; Marina George; my talented writer friend Valerie Cassar; Phyllis Grosskurth; Benita Eisler; Emily Howard; Ethan Lewis Maltby; Mo Pietroni; Peter Collinson; Steve Disleris-Beck; Barbara van Minnen; Allan Barr; Stephen Hewett; Dave Pickering; Kevin Waters; Melvyn Lesser; Patrick Carter; Alan Woodward; Julie Merry; Valerie Chouman; Andre Israel; Pritul Khagram; Amy Cohen; Jane Young; Kate Halliwell; Mike Waddington; Giles Halliwell; Elton Butcher; David Davies; Michael McCaw; Richard Wilcox; Anthony Adolph; Mark George; Diane Scrivens; Mark Bonthrone; Mark Stanton; Sheila Ableman; Zoe Killackey; Jovanka Houska IM; Stuart Conquest GM; Paul Crampton; Andrew Stucken; my brother Rupert Essinger and Joe Mooney; Wendy Mooney.

My thanks also to Eddie Jephcott, Jacqueline Rifai, Alex Rifai, Annie Strahm and Sharon and Zoe Retter for acting so well in the read-through of *Ada's Thinking-Machine*, my screenplay about Ada. I would additionally like to express my gratitude to my optician Kieran Minshull of L.K. Leon & Co, the eye surgeon Mr Wallace Poon and also to Dr Simon Ellis, who was my doctor for 27 years until his retirement in 2013.'

Lightning Source UK Ltd.
Milton Keynes UK
UKHW020119100922
408592UK00003B/55